Because, Mamannie Said So!

Ann Buchanan

Library of Congress Cataloging-In-Publication Data

This book is dedicated to my mother Savannah Obera Davis Freeman 11/11/1925 – 3/26/2017

Mama moved in with me in 2010 when she was eighty-four, I think. After recovering from stage III breast cancer, it was the best thing that ever happened to me at that time. It was such a blessing to have my mother living with me. We were so much alike. We enjoyed the same things cooking, baking and antiquing to name a few. She taught me so much quilting, gardening etc. Every day when we were having dinner, after I came in from work, mama would tell me old family stories. She also taught me how to prepare some of her old family recipes. For example, her mother's more than 100 years old egg pie recipe. It is difficult to get it to come out right unless you know the special technique which she taught me well. After mama passed, I decided to write down those stories and publish them in her honor. This book is also dedicated to Mamannie. Annie Bruce Jones Davis 1896-1989 my very very special grandmother. Because she said never let this Davis family go down this is my way of honoring her wishes.

The George and Annie Davis family is a big, loving, southern, African American family made up of mostly cousins. We have one aunt left at the time of this publishing, Aunt Willie Mae Davis Norwood

This book contains stories and some pictures about my grandparents, their parents, my aunts and uncles; some of their grandchildren and other writings. Also, some old family recipes with updates. There will be a sequel about the grandchildren and other generations. It will also include additional family recipes and remixes of the old recipes.

Thank you for reading my book.

"BECAUSE MAMANNIE SAID SO"

A message to her Family

I am Mamannie, granny to some. You already know how much I love my family. I leave these instructions for you. Especially to those that do not know me. I am a leaf that has fallen from the family tree; however, don't grieve for me because new leaves will always come as the older leaves fall away. I may be gone but I will never be forgotten because I will always be alive in your hearts. Nurture your new leaves. Direct their paths in the right way. I am leaving you lots of love and very very specific instructions to keep this family strong.

Share my memories, my pictures, my funny sometimes sentimental stories. Pass on my delicious recipes; my 100-year-old egg pie recipe, my cakes, pies, chow chow and pear preserve recipes, etc. Pass them down from generation to generations. Teach your children how to make them, which means that you also have to know how to prepare them. Do whatever it takes to help the family stay together. Davis family, I am counting on you to carry our family on into the future.

To our next generations to come; understand who you are; where you came from, know your family history. Our family DNA is flowing through your veins. Recognize our tremendous strength, daring courage and amazing power that reside inside of you. You are standing on the strong backs of your ancestors; their extensive experience, vast Knowledge and extraordinary wisdom passed on to you. Family history is so very important. Research it, cherish it, preserve it and pass it on. To our new strong Davis family tree leaves, we are counting on you to carry the Davis family on into the future.

As I, Mamannie always said, don't ever let this family go down.

Davis family, stay together, communicate regularly and be dedicated to each other.

Worship and fellowship with each other; work and play together. If one of you should fall down, all of you pick them up and get them back on their feet. Support, love and be close to one another, keep the family strong. Family tree leaves, I am counting on you to carry on. I am counting on you! Don't let Granny down.

Each Davis family line all ten of you, I am counting on you to take this family into the future. Don't ever stop celebrating my life; keep my name on your lips, and I will always be with you in your memories and in your hearts. Be strong family; hold on to family love; for love is the glue that will keep you connected and see you through tough times. I am counting on you to carry the family on.

And when you come to the end of your earthly journey, when you are the leaf that has fallen from the family tree and you cross over old chilly Jordan, we, you ancestors, will be there to welcome you back home on the other side.

Family, we are counting on you to carry this strong, Christian African American family into the future.

INTRODUCTION

Mamannie left us, the George and Annie Davis family, strict orders to keep this family together. She said, "no matter what you do, don't let this family go down". This book is my effort to honor her wishes by sharing family history stories, poems, writings and recipes which may help us to know each other better and help us remember those that have passed on.

This book is focused on Pop and Mamannie's generation and a few generations back. Mamannie, also known as granny, is my grandmother on my mother's side of the family. She was the most loving, kind, yet strong-willed smart person that I have ever known. I wish that all of the family could have known her. Annie Bruce Jones

Davis 1896-1989 married our grandfather George Author Davis 1893-1975, December 27, 1913, in Lewisburg TN. She was seventeenth years old.

Cousin Burgess Davis told me that Uncle Lonnie George's older brother, and his father figure, noticed that Mamannie Jones was a beautiful sweet, quit, hardworking, God-fearing young lady. He told young George to pursue her, that she would make a good wife. George followed orders, they fell in love and their marriage lasted sixty-eight years until his death in 1975. They gave birth to twelve children. At her death in 1989 they had sixty-five grandchildren and one hundred and twenty-five great grandchildren.

Uncle Lonnie and George's parents Taylor Zachariah 11-25-1846-1917 and Lucindy Angeline 1852, had nine children. All of them died young other than Thomas Lonnie the oldest child and George Author the youngest. Lonnie and George were very close, and George respected and obeyed him as if he was his parent.

This book is a collection of family stories, pictures, poems, "writings and recipes about the lives of the George and Annie Davis family. An African American family in the rural south, USA. My mother, Savannah Obera Davis Freeman, told me most of these stories. I did some research.

My goal in writing this book is that the stories, pictures, poems and old family recipes will give some insight into the lives of our Davis family for generations to come. There are stories about the antique bed that Pop was born on, the story about Mamannie's mother's death, about Sunday dinners and old as well as updated recipes. If these stories bring back memories, please write your stories down and share them.

These stories have been embellished and enhanced for clarity and entertainment.

STORIES

THE DAY THE TORNADO HIT

Mamannie was always afraid of storms. Anytime it started to rain heavily she would stop everything and have everyone in the house get dressed and sit together quietly. She would sit with us and pray. We did not understand when we were small. As we got older granny would tell us (her children and grandchildren) her story.

It is a family history story about my grandmother Annie Bruce Jones Davis 1896-1989, we call her Mamannie, she was also known as granny to the younger grandchildren.

Her mother, Ida Bruce Johnson Jones, was in her middle thirties and father, Frank Jones, was about forty. Frank's older brother uncle Henry lived in the house next door.

They lived in a segregated African American community in Marshall County TN off Mooresville highway near Webb Rd about fifthly years after slavery.

It was a hot dry day in June of 1908, at about 12 noon. Mamannie was playing outside when she noticed the leaves stirring and the blue ski had a pinkish cast. She begins to feel big drops of rain hitting her face. Suddenly the blue pinkish sky turned pitch black in the middle of the day. Her mother Ida yelled for her to come in quickly, a storm is coming. The neighbors also took cover from the bad storm.

Mamannie told us that she could hear rain pouring down hard, angry gusting wind blowing with loud rumbling sounds of thunder, she saw clamping flashes of lightning shooting across the black sky as she peeped out the window.

Mamannie told us, her mother closed the old, cracked windows and shut the shabby old wood doors. And started praying out loud.

Mamannie was so afraid but also very curious to see what was going on outside. She wanted to see the storm.

She heard loud noises like a railroad train running outside the door. It was in the early afternoon but pitch-black outside. Her mother knew it was serious, they were home alone and

afraid. She told Mamannie to come away from the windows and stay away from the door.

Mamannie was a twelve-year-old very curious young lady that just had to see what was going on outside. She had never seen or heard anything like this before.

She did not know that a tornado was going through. When she touched the frail unlocked door's knob to peak out, the old wood door blew open.

Ida screamed, "no Annie" pushed her down on the bed and fell on top of her.

Mamannie said that she felt the wind carrying her and her mother through the air. She heard her mom say franticly "hold on Annie don't let go of me". She was frozen to her mother as tight as she

17

could. She felt something hit them, but she could not see what it was because she had her eyes closed tight. She was so afraid. She did not hear her mother say anything else. It was over in a matter of minutes.

When the tornado passed the house had blown away and Mamannie and her mama had been blown out in the yard.

Her mother was on top of her but not moving. She struggled to roll her mother over calling her mama, mama she screamed. She was on the mattress. She started moving things out of her way. Screaming for help to the top of her voice she grabbed the mattress and started pulling it with her mother until she got next door to Uncle Henry's house, which was still standing. She was yelling and calling Uncle Henry. Uncle Henry heard her yelling and was already running out to see what had happened. He started to call Ida's name but no response. He checked her out and found a bleeding gash on her head.

Other neighbors came a running and sent for the doctor. They checked her heart, no pulse. She was not breathing. She was pronounced dead when the doctor arrived. Mamannie was devastated. Her mother told her not to open the door, but she did it anyway.

Mamannie felt that this was her fault. The old door did not have a lock and would have opened anyway. But Mamannie did not know that.

She was so sorry. She will never disobey again as long as she lived. However, Mamannie did not know that her house was in the path of the tornado whether she opened the door or not. Mamannie's life changed forever.

I googled the news for tornados in Marshall County in 1908. I found that her mother was one of the victims of the Dixie tornadoes that came through the south Tuesday April 24, 1908, according to the newspaper on file from that day. Her father and brother were not at home when the tornado came through. Mamannie cried uncontrollably. Aunt Josie, her father's sister, was able to console her. She brought her home. Aunt Josie had a little girl named Lou. They comforted and loved Mamannie until she was able to recover from the grief of losing her mother. Although she would never get over it, she learned to live with it.

Her father Frank and her brother James, though grieving also, were able to help Mamannie by showing her a lot of love and attention. She never got over it but was able to go on with her life. She was experiencing symptoms of post-traumatic stress syndrome. She also became a very strict disciplinarian.

Mamannie went to a one room school with her cousin Lou, who was raised as her sister. They walked to school in their home sown dresses made of flour sack cotton and black leather brogan shoes. They carried their lunch pails filled with fresh baked biscuits stuffed with pieces of smoked country sausage, creamy churned butter and sweet home-made pear jam.

According to an article that I pulled up on old African American one room schools, they were taught arithmetic, reading, writing and spelling. The upper classes learned about science, geography and civics.

Pop George told me if he had the education that Mamannie had he could go places. They went from the first to the fifth grade. They also had chores. The boys cleaned the school yard, cut wood and kindled the fire in the potbellied stove during cold weather. The girls cleaned the floor, desk and chairs. And cleaned up after lunch. Mamannie and Lou graduated from the one room school, everyone was so happy for them.

Mamannie was a beautiful dark chocolate brown skinned young lady with lots of thick pretty hair. She was a sweet humble but strong-willed, hard-working Christian young lady. Uncle Lonnie Davis, Pop's oldest brother, noticed her and thought she would be a good wife for George. So, he told him to pursue her. George had noticed her. Beautiful, quiet, and educated. He thought he would never get a woman like Mamannie. But he would not dare disobey Lonnie. Pop was tall thin caramel brown skin with green eyes. He had a head full of curly hair. His mother was half white. He obeyed his big brother and went out to win Mamannie's heart. He talked to her and helped her with her chores. Mamannie thought that he was the most handsome man that she had ever seen. He was funny and made her laugh. They walked to church together. He invited her to Sunday dinner. They went to social gatherings together. In those days they did not have telephones or cars. They all lived in the same area together. They walked everywhere. Pop and Mamannie fell in love and were married on Saturday December 27, 1913. She was 17 years old. The family celebrated Christmas and the marriage. Everyone came to Sunday dinner after Church and the celebration continued. When Pop died in 1975, they had been married 68 years. On their 68th anniversary they asked Pop how it feels to be married 68 years? He said it is the only war that you can stay in 68 years and haven't been killed yet. Mamannie did not pay him any attention. She knew that he loved her. And he knew that she did not play.

According to cousin Burgess, uncle Lonnie's youngest son, they lived with Uncle Lonnie in the beginning. They found a little farmhouse in Lewisburg near Webb Rd. very close to Uncle Lonnie. Popa George was a sharecropper and made a good living to take care of Mamannie. Next year 1914 she gave birth to Uncle Herbert. Then Uncle Thomas and Uncle Jones.

One day when Pop came home for dinner, the noon meal in about 1919. There was a gentle knock on the door. Pop opens the door and to his surprise stood Mrs. Granada Bryant. He invited her to come in. She told them that old man Bryant had died, and her husband had also died with the flu. The 1919 Asian Flu pandemic. So many of the men had died and she needed a good sharecropper.

Because he was a member of the Bryant family, she asked them to move to Bryant station. His mother a slave, was the daughter of old man Jerry Bryant. She offered him a house, rent free and one half of everything he produced. And she offered Mamannie a job ironing at

22

the big house. A very easy job. The offer included a big farmhouse with a very large kitchen. Mamannie was so excited. Mrs. Bryant was very good to them because he was family and she needed him. Popa George did not want to acknowledge that his mother was Jerry Bryant's daughter. He always told everybody that she was full blood "engion" (Indian). But he took the job. Mamannie learned to be an ironing expert and taught mama how to iron like her and mama taught her children. I am still ironing and my grandson also. I did not know that Mamannie had a job ironing at the big house, until mama told me during one of our after-dinner talks, when I asked her if Mamannie ever had a job outside of their home?

Mamannie was always a very strong disciplinarian. She did not tolerate disobedience. Now I know why.

Mamannie always wanted a family. One brother died when he was very young. Her parents died young her mother in the tornado. Uncle Jones told me it is suspected that her father died in the flu pandemic and her older brother James L, Mamannie said he disappeared. She did not know if he died or went North and passed for white. She said her word on the railroad and one day never came home. I did find him in the census report when they were young, I think 1910.

Mamannie gave birth to 12 children, two died one at 13 and one at birth. She loved her big family.

When she died at 94 years old, she had 65 grandchildren, 125 great grandchildren and great-great grandchildren. She left instructions to never let this Davis family go down. And we honor her wishes even today in 2023. Mamannie/granny. We will always love you. I come from a long line of praying women. My great grandmother, my grandmother, my mother, me and my daughter were and are all prayer warriors.

SOME OF MAMA'S EARLY LIFE FAMILY HISTORY

Mama (Savannah Obera Davis Freeman 1925-2017),said that they were a very happy family when she was a little girl. That she did not know that they were poor. They lived in a big farmhouse. Each room was papered with old newspapers. When they were big enough to read, one would find an article on the wall and the other person would have to find it. It was just a fun pass time game that also helped them learn to read. When they were older, they practiced reading and explaining the King James translation of the Bible out loud. They had a lot of love flowing in their home and there is still a lot of love flowing when we get together today.

Her mother, Mamannie (Annie Bruce Jones Davis 1896-1989), also called Granny, was a godly strong woman and a very good cook. She always had a lot of good food cooking. Homemade golden-brown biscuits every morning with homemade fruit jam and crisp on the outside and moist on the inside buttermilk cornbread for dinner every afternoon. Mamannie made homemade dessert every day because they did not eat meat during the week. She made a lot of sides because she wanted her family to have enough to eat, they worked so hard during the day in the fields and that food had to carry them until supper. They were sharecroppers. She always had a big garden full of every vegetable you could imagine. Red tomatoes, yellow corn, green okra, yellow squash, field peas, juicy. plums, sweet peaches, blackberries etc.

She and the girls would can and dry everything that they grew in the garden because they did not have refrigerators nor electricity in the house. And the food had to last from winter to through spring. They dried beans, tomatoes, apples, peaches and berries. They canned green beans, corn, turnip greens, apples, peaches and blackberries. They made chow chow, pickled beets, pickled okra, cucumber sweet and dill pickles. They canned sausage and meat.

The family always went to church.

27

Mama said that Hope Well was the Methodist and the Primitive Baptist church was Mt Piska. The churches met every other Sunday. Pop and Mamannie attended both churches on Sundays. because they did not have church clothing for all ten of the children. Half of the children went to church one Sunday and the other half went the next Sunday. People dressed for church in those days. Pop was a Deacon in the Primitive Baptist church and Mamannie was a Mother of the church. Many times, the Pastor would come from Nashville on Saturday and spend the night at Pop and Mamannie's home.

Mamannie would have a Sunday dinner inviting all of the church. Today the George and Annie Davis family have more than twenty-seven Pastors, Elders, Ministers and Deacons in the family. As well as many ushers and choir members.

Pop and Mamannie taught their children to have a strong Christian family and for them to teach their children to be good Christians. When the Davis family get together at church, whatever you do at your church you do it in the Davis family church service and at Davis family funerals. Some in the choir, some are ushers, Elders and Ministers in the pulpit. Deacons did the devotion and the collection. It is awesome.

There was a one room school. It went to the eighth grade. Mama remembers going to the one room school. The teacher's name was Miss Shell. They walked to school, with the other children in the community, with their lunch pal filled with butter biscuits stuffed with fried country ham and homemade jam. One day Mamannie told them that the census was going to be taken at school that day. Uncle Herbert and Uncle Thomas did not know what the census was and decided to play hooky. They were hiding on the bank about a mile from the school. They saw an airplane flying above them. They started yelling "it's an airplane" they were yelling loud not knowing that Mamannie was in the field nearby and heard them.

They were caught and surprised because Mamannie normally did not work in the field. She made them bring her a switch and she whipped their legs all the way to school. They were about ten and twelve years old and never played hooky again. Mamannie loved them and disciplined them so that they would grow up doing the right thing. None of her children ever went to jail or prison. Mama said she always obeyed her parents because she did not want a whipping. In those days it was okay to spank a child. Spare the rod and spoil the child is what they believed. They did not beat them, but they did spank them.

These are a few stories that mama shared with me about her early family life.

Poppa Georges Table

Stories from gatherings around the George and Annie Davis family table. Popa George was always very good at building furniture, from a young boy, he was always carving, weaving and whittling wood furniture. He and Mamannie live in a large frame farm home on the Bryant station farm where he was a sharecropper and the grandson of the former plantation owner, old man Jerry Bryant. Mamannie did the ironing for the white folks in the big house, and she was very good at it. They loved Mamannie.

In their farmhouse the front room was a bedroom. They had a very large kitchen with a cast iron cooking stove, a pie saver and a cupboard. As his family began to grow, Pop wanted them to set around the kitchen table together talking and eating their meals. So, he set out to build a table for his family.

He called the neighbor men together and told them what he wanted to do. They went to the shied and found old wood left over from building the barn. The long brown oaks planks were strong and beautiful. They glued the planks across and put a clamp on them until the glue set. Then they nailed planks on the bottom side to strengthen the top. The table was six feet wide and eight feet long. They had a lot of friends and family.

Pop and the men secured the legs of the table to the top and began to sand the wood down. Then waxed and buffed it to a bright shine. Pop and the men continued working until they finished the twelve chairs to go with the table.

When he brought the table and chairs in Mamannie sat down at the table with George and started planning a Sunday dinner to celebration the new family table. She was so happy, and he was very proud of himself.

Aunt Savanna, Pop's sister and aunt Berline Pop's aunt helped Mamannie pull the dinner together. They sat around the table and planned what they would serve. They also exchanged the neighborhood gossip. Mostly things that went on in the big house, white folks' troubles. Old master bringing his mulatto children to work in the big house and Mrs. having to look at them all day. The talk of politics thinking that the workers did not have since enough sense to understand what they were talking about. If this table could only talk. The stories it could tell.

They planned to serve hen and dumplings; molasses glanced country ham with buttermilk biscuit. Allspice and butter baked apples, turnip greens with turnip roots, green beans with shelly peas. Fresh fried corn and baked okra with home grown tomatoes. Hot water crackling cornbread, two big twelve-inch egg pies, iced tea and condiments such as chow chow, sweet pickle, beet pickle, onion, tomatoes and cucumbers.

They invited the church, relatives and neighbor. All of the guests brought covered dishes.

Mandy brought dressed eggs. We call them stuffed eggs. Annabelle brought yellow squash casserole.

Mildred and Rita brought fresh fried chicken that they killed, cleaned and fried that morning. Joyce made a big caramel cake and Susanna mad a large double crust fresh peach cobbler. The men brought out Mamannie's blackberry wine.

Mamannie covered the big new wood table with a large white, cotton, freshly starched and ironed tablecloth. Also, beautiful flowers from the garden. The women were in the kitchen preparing the food to serve. Some cut the desserts, some put the vegetables in serving dishes and some cut the meat and put it on a large serving platter. The hen and dumplings went in a large serving bowl. Everything was placed on the long side table. It looked so beautiful. Mamannie always saves back plenty of food for the women and children. Unlike some women that gave them the leftovers. Men and guess were always fed first.

The children were running and playing outside in the side yard near the gardens and flowers. The men were gathered on the long narrow front porch where you could see the ground through the spaces between the planks. Some of the men were sitting in the porch swing, some in cane back chairs, some sitting on the rock steps and some standing. They had a very lively conversation going about the politics of the times. Some of the men were laughing, joking and some arguing as some of them sipped the homemade blackberry wine.

Mamannie called the men to the table. She asked Elder Statton to pray over the food. "Father God, Master, we thank you for this food we are about to receive, good bread, good meat, good people let's eat" amen. They laughed at the prayer as they passed the delicious food, they shared secrets about how to avoid being cheated with the share cropping contract and other community news.

After dinner, the noon meal, the lower end of the table was covered with a smaller cloth covering left over desserts fried pies, corn bread and biscuits. People sat at the upper end of the table and talked about good times and bad time. Uncle Henry told Pop that he was planning on divorcing Aunt Tilley because she is pregnant with twins by Billy Joel. Pop told him to forgive her and raise them as his own. They sent Billy Joel North to work in the automotive factories. They never heard of him again.

One day Dr. Bass came by to talk with Pop and Mamannie. They sat down at the table, and he told them that he could not do anything to help their twelve-year-old daughter Lucille. She had

Tuberculosis and is dying. If he could have gotten to her sooner maybe he could have helped her. The tears, the fear, broken hearts and prayers that flowed from this table. If this table could only talk. The stories it could tell.

They sat around this table to balance their budget. Some year good and some years not so good. But they always made it with the help of the Lord. They sat at that table and offered that budget up to the Lord in prayer and He always worked it out.

My mother told me that, one-year Pops invited the Primitive Baptist church from Nashville for Sunday dinner. Pop was having an inappropriate relationship with the Pastor's sister. Yes, Deacon Davis was having an affair, and he knew better. She came with the church to Sunday dinner at his home. She sat at the table with the rest of the guess. My mother was there helping Mamannie serve the guess. Some of the Mothers has already told Mamannie about this woman. Mamannie called my mama to the garden, let's get you some vegetables to take home. When she got out there Mamannie told her about the girl friend. Mama was so mad that she wanted to go in there and pull her away from that table and beat her down. But Mamannie said no. You pray for both of them. It took all that mama had in her not to attack this woman. How could she dare set her big ugly feet under Mamannie's table, mama said. Mamannie was a humble kind sweet Lady who believed in taking everything to God in prayer. Some years later when Pops was sick and knew he was dying. He confessed it all to Mamannie. She said he told her that after that dinner the woman was so ashamed that she stopped seeing him. Prayer will surely change things. Give it over to the Lord and He will surely work it out.

I don't know what ever happened to that table. After they retired and moved to a small home in the city, the table was too big for the new smaller kitchen. There were so many good memories and some not so good memories, around that table. If that table could only talk, the stories it could tell.

HAPPY 18TH BIRTHDAY TO
MY DAUGHTER NICOLE!!! I
LOVE YOU!!!

IF POP'S BED COULD TALK

I f only Pop's bed could talk the stories it would tell. It was June 10, 1852, one of the enslaved women Angeline Tidwell was in the middle of giving birth to my great grandmother Lucindy Angeline on Pop Georges bed. According to oral history she was the plantation master's concubine. He put the bed in her slave hut so he could be comfortable. She, Angeline Tidwell, gave birth to his six children by her on that bed.

I was a little girl about five or six years old in about 1953. On Sundays once a month or so, my parents, JW Freeman 1926-1994 and Savannah Obera Davis Freeman 1925-2017, would take us to see our grandparents. My mother's parents George Author Davis 1893-1975 and Annie Bruce Jones Davis 1896-1989. They lived outside of Columbia TN on Bryant Station farm. Later they moved to North Water St. in Columbia TN when they were too old to sharecrop. We would leave their home and go to my father' s parents Willie Hatton Freeman 1998-1981 and Annie Williams Freeman 1904- 1997 in Belfast TN about thirty miles from the Alabama line. We lived in Nashville TN.

Walking into the front door of Popa George and Annie's rustic farm home, the first thing that I notice was a big brown bed that looked like, to my young eyes, it took up most of the front room. Well, in a way it did take up most of the front room because the room was so small.

Even though it looked like a great big bed in their front room it really was a small three quarters bed. Three quarters the size of a full-size bed. The bed was shorter and narrower than a full-size bed but bigger than a twin-size bed.

It was customary for the front room to be a bedroom in the black community. The families were very large, and houses were small in many cases. Family and friends visiting Pop and Mamannie, gathered in the kitchen around their big, family table that Pop built, which was used for meals and family gatherings.

Pop's bed was always very fascinating to me. It was not the age or rich brown color of the wood or the small intricate carvings on the tall six-foot square headboard that fascinated me. What I loved most was the stories about the bed's history. Every time we visited; I would always ask Pop to tell me the stories about his bed. I really did not understand the history at that time. And I am surprised that I remembered every word that he told me. I can still hear him telling the story in my head.

He was always happy to tell me the stories again and again. Looking at me with a big smile on his thin, sun damaged, brown, wrinkled face with sparkling grey eyes and white eyebrows. Chewing his tobacco as we rocked in his big squeaky, wood rocking chair, which was also in the tight front room between the antique dresser and the foot of the three quarter's bed, he repeated "remember this, I was born on this bed and my mother Lucindy Angeline Marish Davis in 1852 was born on this bed. And all twelve of my children were born from 1915-1930 on this bed. And all of my mother's children were born on this bed. That is why it is so special. I promised him that I would never forget.

When I started studying family history, it dawned on me what he was trying to tell me. I was in my sixties. What a magnificent gift. I still wonder how he knew that I would cherish this bed.

In those days children were born at home instead of in the hospital.

Aunt Trudy, the little old white-haired midwife would always come when it was time for Mamannie to give birth on this bed.

She would prepare the bed with old newspapers that had been saved up for the last few weeks used to dispose of the placenta which was buried in the field, old sheets and old cloth flour sacks bags that had been washed and prepared to protect the mattress. This was before we had plastic. And when the time came to deliver, after hours of labor, she would give birth to the baby.

My mother told me when Mamannie was about to give birth to her, cutN ExieB and cutN Lillian, Mamannie's cousins came to be with her and the midwife. They came to help with the other children and to keep the house while Mamannie was recovering from giving birth. She was the seventh child. The new mother could not touch her feet to the floor, wash her hair or bathe for seven days after the baby was born.

The women that came to help would help bath her and the baby in the bed. Then she would nurse the baby, rest and sleep for seven days.

Mama said Mamannie told her when she was born, she had already started labor during the night. The next morning while leaving for work to the farm's cotton fields, Pop kissed Mamannie and told her to remember to name the baby Savanna after his only sister and his aunt if it is a girl. They did not know the baby's sex in advance of its birth in 1925. Pop sent Uncle Jones to go get cutN ExieB and cutN Lillian because he had long legs and could run fast as well as they did not have telephones. Aunt Trudy the midwife had been there all night. It was time for the pushing to begin. She would take deep breaths then push with all of her strength until they heard the screaming cry of the newborn baby. Aunt Trudy cleaned her up and announced that it was a girl.

Aunt Berline Pop's aunt and also came to help with the six other children. While waiting, Aunt Berline would bake ginger molasses tea cakes. Lots and lots of tea cakes. She would give the children one each from each batch baked. Aunt Lillian cooked a big pot of field peas with country ham hocks, a gallon jars of canned turnip greens were opened and heated, a big pan of nutmeg and vanilla laced candied yams and two large black 12 oz cast iron skillets of cornbread. She also made a gallon of sweet tea. She wanted a really good dinner for the family to enjoy and celebrate the birth of their new sister. And she could really cook. Everyone was rejoicing except Pop.

After they saw that the beautiful baby was a little girl, they named her Savannah as Pop had requested, then cutN ExieB told Mamannie to add Obera to her name, that she looked like an Obera, a beautiful little African Queen. Mamannie agreed, not knowing that Pop would be so mad about adding Obera to her name.

When Pop came home very tired, hungry, and thirsty from working in the fields all day but very excited to welcome his new child. The midwife told Pop that they had a beautiful baby girl. That her name is Savannah Obera. "Obera" he yelled; I told you to name her Savannah. Obera, he was so mad that they added the name Obera on to Savanna that he felt steam coming from his ears, he told Mamannie that you knew that I wanted her named after my only sister. With an ugly frown on his face he stated, I will never call her that name. So, he gave her the nickname, Mutt and he called her Mutt until he died.

If only Pop's old bed could tell all of its amazing stories. Both the good and the bad, it could be a New York Times bestselling book.

I was always so happy to spend time with Pop and hear those old family stories about his bed.

As we look back in history about this bed, Pop's mother Lucindy Angeline Bryant called Angie was born on the bed in 1852. The bed belonged to her mother Angeline Tidwell, my second great grandmother, who was a slave born in 1825 on the Bryant plantation. Angeline Tidwell was a beautiful young mulatto slave woman and her master fell in love with her. She became his concubine.

Angeline Tidwell was listed as Jerry Bryant's wife on the census report in 1870 I am told by one of her DNA descendants. Angeline was his slave so they could not have been married. It appeared that they did have a secret romantic relationship. It was passed down by word of mouth that he gave her the bed that their six children were born on so that she could be comfortable in her slave hut. Especially when he visited her.

I suspect it was more so that he could be comfortable. I have no idea how old the bed was when he gave it to her. Tom and David

Bryant, twin boys, were born to them in 1844 on the bed when she was nineteen years old. Neil was born 1850 six years later on the bed. Lucindy Angeline, my great grandmother, was born in 1852 on the bed, Jeff was born in 1863 eleven years later and Jackson was born between Jeff and Eller all on the bed.

Jackson was not Jerry Bryant's child, he belonged to her husband Anthony Davis who she married in 1864 after she was freed from slavery. Eller her last son was born in 1870 was Jerry Bryant's child and was born on the bed.

Anthony Davis was not related to the Taylor Davis family. If this bed could only talk. I am sure we will learn the rest of the story. This information came from family history passed down verbally an old family.

Tree sent to me by a DNA cousin.

Angeline Tidwell gave the bed to Angie (Lucindy Angeline), her daughter, when she married Taylor Zachariah Davis.

All of their children were born on that bed. His only sister Savanna 1879, his brothers Thomas Lonnie 1881, Virgil R 1884, John E 1887, Sammie A 1890 and Taylor George Author 1893. All of the siblings died young other than Uncle Lonnie the oldest child and Pop the youngest child.

Lucindy Angeline gave the bed to my grandfather George Author, her last-born child and the grandson of the plantation owner Jerry Bryant, when he married my grandmother Annie Bruce Jones Davis December 27, 1914.

Popa George left me the bed at his death, but I did not know it until after he died. I was so surprised.

Pop and Mamannie slept in that bed together for sixty-eight years. She gave birth to twelve children on that bed.

The years passed. I had stopped asking Pop about the bed. Popa George had been sick for a few years now. Pop and Mamannie moved from the Bryant Station farm on the edge of Columbia TN to a little home in Columbia TN city limits on North Water St. They were no longer able to share crops. They lived on social security. And the adult children helped them. In August 1975 Popa George had a heart attack and died while resting in his bed. He was eighty-five years old. I was twenty-seven years old, grown and married when he died. After the

47

funeral. Mamannie moves in with Aunt Rachel and her family, because she was too old to live in the tiny house alone.

One day about a week after the funeral, Mamannie called my mother and told her that Pop wanted me to have his bed after he passed on. That I should come and get the bed. How did he know that I would cherish the bed and its memories? And carefully pass it on.

I was so surprised. I could not believe it. He had a huge family and he left me his historically famous bed. I am so grateful.

It took me some time to get the bed to my home. My brother Jerry picked it up and had it for a while. When I finally got the bed, I ordered a new three-quarter size mattress, box springs and sheets for it. The mattress and box springs had to be custom made. Also had the wood cleaned with fine oil furniture polished.

No one sleeps on this almost two-hundred-year-old family heirloom now.

It is an old brown oak bed with a six feet high headboard and a four feet foot board. I don't think that it is so pretty. It is pure history.

Sometimes, I lay on the bed and think about its stories and see them in my mind. I thought, "how did they sleep in such a small bed for sixty-eight years?" Pop was tall and thin Mamannie was short and plump.

If this bed could tell its stories, it would be a bestselling book. This bed has made it through slavery in the early 1800's generation to generation and even today in 2023 it is still standing.

Now, what do I do with this bed when I pass on. It is so full of family history. I have to be sure that the person that I leave it to will have the same passion that I had. I plan to leave this bed to my daughter. She says that she would cherish it. I have instructed her to try to keep the bed and its stories in the family.

If my grandchildren don't want it, she will give it to someone else in the Davis family blood line that will also cherish it and its stories. Or it could be donated to the African American history museum.

I have written the bed's history and stories and taped it to the back of the bed. So that the history of this bed will live on with the bed. I am also going to publish this story in a book of family history stories. The end.

SUNDAY DINNER

The field slaves were whispering and laughing. The news went all over the plantations. Sunday Dinner at Deacon Davis's house. Some of the slaves had to get permission to travel to the next plantation. Some had to walk one hours to get there. Every family begin preparing. The slaves did not have much to celebrate. They had a brief church service on Sundays, they participated in the celebrations at the big house and funerals. But every first Sunday in each quarter, if they were lucky, the slaves would be allowed to have Sunday Dinner together.

It was not only plenty of good food at Sunday dinner but, the men shared the news about the Underground Railroad and about life living in the North. It is not all that it was cracked up to be. It is very cold, and life is very hard in the black ghetto.

The women talked about who was pregnant again; how to take care of your body after giving birth, don't let your feet touch the floor for seven days. You must breast feed your baby. They also talked about how to make your food taste really good put the seasoning to it. And, how to make your husband happy by never refusing him love making, even if it is most every day. The older women taught the younger women. They taught them respect for their elders and good manners, forgiveness and to always tell the truth. As well as to work hard and be honest.

Sunday dinners were so important because it was the only time the enslaved could get together with their family and friends.

So many enslaved families were separated because they were sold to other slave owners. It was a few hours to forget their situations and just enjoy each other. It was a tradition that went on from generation to generation.

Pop and Mamannie Davis, my grandparents, had Sunday dinner about every first Sunday in the quarter also when the weather permitted.

Sometimes every other month depending on the weather. They had their adult children and their families; some of the church members and some of the neighbor to get together and break bread.

Mamannie was up at four o'clock AM Sunday morning looking in the hen house to determine which hens she was going to kill for hen and cornbread dressing for this Sunday dinner. She selected two big fat hens and rang their necks with all her strength until their necks separated from their bodies. After they stopped jumping and flopping around the yard, she drained the blood and put the hens in hot salt water, she then plucked the feathers off and soaked the hens in a special cold seasoned brine solution.

The brine contained water, salt, sugar, hot peppers, garlic, onions celery, carrots, bell pepper, rosemary, sage and thyme. She boiled them for a while then slow baked them in her wood burning oven until they were completely done.

Ida Bruce and Mutt, my mother, had picked, washed and started two bushels of turnip greens cooking with two large smoked ham hocks. Hazel and Willie Mae peeled the sweet potatoes, seasoned them with sugar, nutmeg, vanilla, butter, salt and cinnamon then put them in the oven to cook down until the syrup was thick and candied.

Mamannie boiled two dozen brown hen eggs to stuff. She prepared them with her homemade mayonnaise and sweet pickle relish.

Aunt Virginia brought turnips and roasted pork roast, a mess of field peas, a butter roll and four vanilla and lemon-flavored chess pies. Aunt Ida Mae brought sweet and sour meatloaf, fried corn, baked okra and her specialty chocolate meringue pies. Aunt Lou brought brown sugar spiced, glazed baked ham, baked buttermilk corn bread and sweet lemon iced tea. Mamannie pulled out canned pickled cucumbers, beets, okra and chow chow catchup. Aunt Frances, aunt WillieMae, and Aunt Rachel set the tables and prepared the food to serve.

Mamannie called, "dinner is served. Y'all come and get it". Papa George said grace with, "Good God, good meat, come all, let's eat. Amen." The men who were outside engaged in a heated political conversation, came inside to the big brown dinner table that Pop built. The older women and guest also sat at the table. The younger women served the meal and the children played outside until the adults were finished. The younger women would clear the table, wash the dishes and reset the table for them and the women and children to eat. Some brought in water and heated it on the cast iron stove, some washed and others dried the dishes, and some reset the table. They laughed and talked while working. It was so much fun to be with the family and friends one more time. After dinner they started their long trip back to their various homes. Some came from Nashville. Some lived in Lewisburg and some in Culleoka, Columbia and Mt. Pleasant TN.

Sunday Dinners continued generation after generation. Pop and Mamannie continued having family and friends for Sunday Dinner for many years. As the grandchildren got older and Pop and Mamannie retired from share cropping and moved to the city, the new house was too small to have everyone and their families for Sunday dinners. So, my mother Savannah Obera planned to get everyone, all of her siblings and their families, together to have dinner in the park after church. Every family brought lots of good food.

It was the first George and Annie Davis family reunion, but they did not know it at the time. No one remembers the year. They continued having family get togethers on holidays and Sundays as the weather permitted.

Then the family in Nashville started to get together on Sundays. They would bring covered dishes to each other's homes. It was so much fun. And the family in Lewisburg came together as well as in Columbia.

The entire family began to get together once a year.

As my mother's children grew up, mama started having Sunday dinners with her children and their families. As did all of her sisters and brothers.

After she settled in Lewisburg and joined St. James PB church, she started having Sunday dinner in her small two-bedroom apartment. Most every Sunday after church, mama would have Sunday dinner. Mama would cook a lot of good food on Saturday and finish up on Sunday morning before Sunday school started. She would invite all of the church, family and neighbors for Sunday dinner. Sometimes people would bring covered dishes. Most of the time she cooked everything. There were people everywhere, in her apartment, on the porch, in the yard and on the sidewalk. There was nothing like mama's Sunday dinners.

After mama moved to Nashville with me, we begin to have Sunday dinners, it was always so much fun. About twice a month. I would cook up turnip greens sweet potatoes, chicken and meat loaf on Saturday night and so many other dishes as well as a dessert. Cobblers, pies and caramel cakes. Mama would call all of her children and their families over for Sunday dinner. The young children would run and play outside. The other children were on their electronic games, the men in the den and the women in the front room. When the food was ready, mama would call everyone in to pray over the food and for the family. And then there is the wait in line to get the food. It was served buffet style. We would always have to say let the seniors go first.

Then everything would get quiet, and the family was enjoying the food. The days of being served at the table was passed and gone.

THE WHOOPIN'

Thick dark red syrup was bubbling around the edges of the large black cast iron skillet when Mamannie removed the golden brown blackberry cobbler from the wood burning Stove oven. She placed it on the kitchen window ledge to cool. It was a beautiful, sunny day in late summer on the Bryant farm in Columbia TN. The year was sometime during the early 1930s.

Hollis Jones was chasing butterflies in the wildflowers on the side of the house while visiting with Mamannie. He began to smell the sweet inviting aroma of the blackberry cobbler cooling on the giant kitchen window ledge that Pop George built for Mamannie to cool her delicious scratch made pies. It smelled so good that he could not wait until dinner as he was instructed.

Five-year-old HollisJones waited until Mamannie went to her garden in the backyard, to pick vegetables for the afternoon meal. He went through the big open kitchen and climbed on to the counter with the enormous window ledge. He picked up a big metal mixing spoon with his little hands and filled it with golden brown crust, sweet blackberries and thick red juice.

He ran to the weather-beaten picket fence on the back side of the leaning grey barn to take a bite of the delicious cobbler. Lost in the moment of eating his first scrumptious bite, getting sweet red juice on his face, dripping on to his nice clean shirt, khaki shorts and brand-new snickers. "Ooh Ooh" he heard something, they were footsteps, and he felt a familiar presence; he stopped chewing his delicious mouthful of sweet cobbler and looked up. There stood Mamannie with her wrinkled brown hands on her short wide hips. Her dark brown eyes piercing down at him. He could have wet his pants.

HollisJones knew better than to get into Mamannie pies. She did not allow anyone to get into her pies before dinner, not even herself. She had at least twelve hungry people to provide two servings each of her after dinner desserts. She wanted to be sure that everyone got enough to eat since they did not eat meat through the week. They only eat meat on Sunday. That is why Sunday dinner was so special. Mamannie was a very loving, kind, strong-willed, grey-haired grandmother that did not tolerate disobedience.

She reluctantly instructed him to bring her a switch. With tears streaming down his face, dreading the impending spanking, as he broke the long thin switch from a bush, he thought to himself, why did I do it, as he took the switch to her.

Mamannie lightly whipped his legs and reminded him again, never get into her pies. The switching hurt her heart more than it did his legs.

HollisJones, crying with hurt feelings more than pain from the whoopin, waited for Pop George who was coming in from the fields tired, hungry ready to eat dinner, (the noon meal). He went, crying to Popa George Mamannie whooped me" big crocodile tears flowing. Popa George was so angry, he could feel steam coming from his ears. He was furious about his first-born grandbaby getting a whoopin! He felt that HollisJones was special. Pop George thought he was too good to get a spanking.

Everything does not require a whoopin Pop George shouted at Mamannie.

He grabbed Hollisjones up to his chest kissing his tears and assuring him that everything is going to be alright. Pop rocked him in his strong muscular arms until he fell asleep.

Mamannie strongly affirmed to Popa George that a child must be raised to be obedient. He must be taught right from wrong, or he will bear the consequences in life. Spare the rod and spoil the child she stated. She thought to herself, I did what I had to do. She stood up for what she believed in. George would just have to get over it.

HollisJones Davis is the oldest grandson of George Davis 1893-1975 and Annie Jones Davis 1896-1989. He is the son of George Thomas and Virginia Wilkes Davis and my 1st cousin. He had a little sister Frances Irene. He was about 5 years old when he got the whoopin. He was tall and thin with chocolate colored skin, with big bright dark brown eyes. He was a happy go lucky, curious little boy who loved spending time with his grandparents Pop George and Annie Davis. He is about 80 years old today. Had a 20-year career in the military and never ever got into any trouble again that we know of Thanks to the whoopin.

HOMECOMING DINNER

Popa George, Hubert, Thomas, Jones, uncle George Jones , uncle Lonnie and grandpa Taylor sitting around the big brown rectangle kitchen table that Pop built for his large Homecoming dinners.

There is laughter, talking and sharing of the community news while waiting on the delicious Homecoming dinner being prepared by Mamannie, aunt Savannah, Aunt Berline, cutN ExieB, Ida Bruce, Lucille and Obera.

The deep rich aroma of turnip greens with smoked country ham hocks from the smokehouse cooking. It smells so good. There is nothing like the aroma of big African American families preparing dinner.

You could see the big pot of chicken and dumplings simmering on the back burner of the cast iron stove. Mamannie killed a big fat hen, removed the feathers and innards. Soaked the hen in salt water for an hour, then boiled it with celery, onion, bell pepper salt and pepper until the meat was falling off the bone. She put eight cups of flour in a bowl with a tablespoon of salt and enough broth and fat to make a firm ball. She floured the bread board and rolled out the dumplings, cutting them into long strips. Then drop broken strips of dough into boiling broth. She put the deboned hen back into the pot and let it simmer on the stove for hours.

There was also a big pan of orange-colored sweet potatoes laced with sugar, warm nutmeg and sweet vanilla topped with golden marshmallows. There was also a pot of dried seasoned field peas simmering on the stove.

Ida Bruce was frying golden, crispy hot water corn pones in the large black cast iron pot full of bacon grease. Lucille was slicing molasses and black pepper coated country ham that Pop cured in the smoke house. while Obera pulled out the jars of chow chow, pickled okra and blackberry jam that Mamannie, and the girls canned during the end of summer when the vegetables and fruits were in abundance.

The food was ready to serve. Mamannie interrupted the lively conversations flowing around the big brown rectangle table that Pop built, as they sipped on sweet lemon-flavored home brewed iced tea.

The women piled the delicious food on the table. Mamannie instructed George to bless the food before it gets cold.

There were two big twelve inch, made from scratch, apple pies cooling in the cast iron skillets in the large window seal.

A week before this Sunday dinner Pop called his sons and neighbor men together to build a kitchen table. They had wide flat planks left over from the barn raising. The planks were two by eight inches wide by six feet long. They took five planks, glued and nailed them together. Added six legs one on each corner and to in the middle for support and sanded the wood until it was silky smooth. They stained and sealed the wood. By Saturday Pop's table was ready to be brought into the kitchen. He was so proud.

Every important conversation was discussed at this table. If this table could talk. It would tell all of the family secrets.

Some of the sharecroppers from the other farms did not get paid what was agreed. However, Pop always got paid every penny he was owed and then some because he was the plantation owner's grandson, and they all knew it. If only this table to talk.

Pop told the family that Mrs. Granitta Bryant asked him to come to the farm and share crops for her. Some of the Bryant men had died and they were short of workers. Pop agreed. They gave him a home, one third of everything he made for the farm and anything else they needed to get started. They gave Mamannie a job ironing in the big house according to mama.

One evening some of the young white Bryant men asked Pop to come to a family gathering. Pop declined, he refused to acknowledge that he was a grandchild. He refused the land and the house they offered him.

Weddings were planned at the table, pregnancies and funerals were planned. Bible study and church business were discussed, and all of the family meals were required to be served at this table.

POP'S BURIAL MONEY

Papa George died in 1975. He had a $300 life insurance policy that he paid 25 cent per week for fifty years. The cost of a funeral in Columbia TN was about $800 in 1975. Pop had already paid for his Mamannie and granddaughter Barbara's burial site at Hope Well AME church family cemetery.

This is one of the family stories mama told me during one of our evening after dinner talks. I actually remember some of this story. I was twenty-eight years old when Pop died. Mama got a call to come home pop was in the emergency room. Mama left work at Parkview hospital where she was a nurse technician and went to Columbia TN. She lived in Nashville.

Mama got to the hospital in Columbia and asked what room is George Davis in? She had planned to tell him to get up out of that bed and get to work to get a big laugh out of him. They looked him up and told her he is at V K Ryan funeral home. Mama said that she was devastated it took her breath and her legs began to get weak. After she got herself together, she life the hospital and went to their family home where the family had gathered. They did not tell her that he died because they did not want her upset while driving.

Both Pop and Mamannie had a three-hundred-dollar life insurance policies that they had been paying a quarter per week for many years, at least fifty. I am sure they had paid in much more than three hundred dollars over the years, especially with the interest accrued.

They were fully aware that three hundred dollars were not enough to cover their burial. However, they had a big family to help cover the cost of the funeral. Pop had already paid for the burial plots, at Hope Well AME church family cemetery. He paid for him, Mamannie and one of the grandchildren Barbara Lucille. Because they were raising her.

Pop had a special pair of overalls. He would never let Mamannie wash or even touch them. His special pair of overalls had about twenty pockets. Pockets at the waistline, little pockets on top of those pockets, pockets on the side of the lower legs and pockets on the back with little pockets on them. Then he had added pockets pinned on the inside of the overalls.

The pockets were all stuffed with something. It may have been money. Mamannie knew that something was going on with those overalls but, she just let them alone as he requested. Pop had been in the hospital in Nashville. He had heart trouble. He was doing some better since he got home and was taking his medications as ordered. He was eighty-two years old.

Aunt Rachel had been checking on them frequently since Pop had been so sick. She called and came by to lay eyes on them a few times   a   day. One afternoon while alone with Mamannie Pop took his last breath. It broke Mamannie's heart. A while after his funeral, Mamannie was finally able to wash his special overalls before giving them away to charity. When she picked up his overalls, they felt heavier than normal, and she saw a twenty-dollar bill sticking out of a pocket. As she began looking in the twenty pockets of those special overalls, she found money in all twenty pockets. There were twenties, fifties and hundred-dollar bills. He had saved over two thousand dollars he had been saving for a few years. All of her children and grandchildren had already paid the cost of the funeral.

Mamannie was so surprised. She thought it might be a couple of hundred dollars in his overalls not over two thousand. She called Aunt Rachel and told her. She lived around the corner and came a running. Two thousand dollars was a lot of money in nineteen seventy-five. It solved a lot of problems. Money was very short so that money helped her get the house cleared so that she could move in with Aunt Rachel and family. And it left her some money to live on for a while. Mamannie never worked outside her home accept when she was first married. She did the ironing for the big house during the years, when they were sharecroppers on the Bryant Station farm. She would have to depend on Pop's small social security check now that he is gone.

After counting all of the money. Mamannie sat down and began to think about the last few months. Pop had spent a couple of weeks in Vanderbilt hospital due to a massive heart attack. When he came home, she gladly took care of him.

70

Mamannie said it was her duty as his wife. He was so weak. Pop George was eighty-two years old and had a feeling that his time on earth was winding up.

She said he told her as a Deacon in the church he knew that he had to repent for the mistakes he had made during their sixty-eight-year marriage.

Mamannie thought about the afternoon she was rubbing his back; he began to talk to her about affairs that he had been involved in over the years.

One of them was an affair with the Pastors sister. When the Primitive Baptist church from Nashville came to their home in Columbia for Sunday dinner, this woman came to their home and sat at their dinner table. He confessed to her that he snuck out butter, eggs, meat and canned goods from the house and gave them to her. Mamannie already knew about the affair. The other mothers at the church told her. She decided to give it to the Lord and say nothing to him about it. Pop asked Mamannie to forgive him? That he was sorry for his infidelities. She did not deserve it. She was a very good wife. Mamannie said that she told him that she was a

Christian and Mother of the church, she had to forgive him. But she did not have to like it. She told him that he needs to ask the Lord to forgive him. And that he should be ashamed of himself, a father and a Deacon.

She thought that the money he lifted helped her to get over the anger she felt about the way he treated her. Overall, they had a good marriage, but he did have some periods of infidelity which was not good. She was happy that he did understand that she would need some money after he passed so he started saving. This was one of the ways that   he   showed   his   deep   love   for   her.

WHO WAS LUCINDY MARSH?

Uncle Lonnie, Thomas Lonnie Davis, was Pop Arthur Davis' (my grandfather) oldest brother. Pop was the last-born child of the family. All of the children between Uncle Lonnie who was the oldest child and Pop died young.

When uncle Lonnie died his wife wrote on his death certificate that his mother was Lucindy Marsh Davis. Father was Taylor Zachariah Davis.

We knew for a fact that Pop's mother was Angeline Bryant Davis. We were told that Uncle Lonnie and Pop had the same mother and father.

I ask my uncles and aunts about Lucindy Marsh, no one ever heard of her. I began to ask my cousins if anyone knew why Uncle Lonnie's mother was listed, by his wife, as Lucindy Marsh on his death certificate? No one knew the answer. We were told that Grandpa Taylor was only married one time and that was to Angeline. I looked at the census report for 1870. Lucindy Marsh Davis was listed as negro born 1854. The children were all listed under her and Taylor. Angeline Bryant Davis was also listed in the 1880 census as mulatto born 1852. She and Taylor lived with Zachariah Davis Taylor's father who was sixty-five and head of the household; no children listed the age was not correct.

It was so confusing. I call cousin.

Burgess Davis, Uncle Lonnie's youngest child and the only child still living. He only remembers Grandma Angie. He never heard of Lucindy, he stated.

One day Barbara Davis Draine, my first cousin, aunt Hazel Davis Tucker's daughter (my mother Savannah Obera Davis Freeman's sister) was at Uncle Jones 101 birthday celebration. I asked her if she ever heard of Lucindy Marsh Davis? She said I have heard of that name. She had written down some family roots that pop told her, but she would have to go home to look for it. She had some papers that she needed to look through. I was so excited. However, she got home and could not find where she wrote the I formation down.

One day about six months later she called me and told me that she found the Bible that she wrote the roots information in. She thought that it had been on a piece of paper. She said Pop told her that Lucindy is Angeline's first name. They are the same person. She was a mulatto. Born in 1852. They called her Angie Davis. Mamannie wrote in her bible that George's parents were Zack and Angie Davis. Zack was Taylor Zachariah Davis. He was named after his father Zachariah Davis born 1832. The information in the 1870 census was not correct.

Angeline Bryant's mother was Angeline Tidwell born 1825 an enslaved person. She had five or six children with Jerry Bryant the plantation owner. Lucindy Angeline was one of the six children. After the emancipation proclamation Angeline Tidwell married Anthony Davis (not in the Taylor Davis family) and had one child.

Then in 1870 she had another with Jerry Bryant. I do not know what happened to her husband. I am told that he died. It appears that

Angeline Tidwell went back to Jerry Bryant and had another child with him.

Family oral history says she was his concubine and he loved her very much.

- Lucindy Angeline was a Bryant. We do not know where Marsh came from. My grandmother told us that George's mother was Angeline Marsh Bryant before she married Taylor (Zac) Davis, Georges' father

UNCLE ZEKE ROBBED

Uncle Ezkiel Marlow 1930-2019 was married to aunt Frances Davis Marlow 1930-2014. She was my mother's, Savannah Obera Davis Freeman 1925-2017, little sister. Zeke was short for Ezekiel. He came from Mt. Pleasant TN and moved to Nashville after he married Aunt Frances in 1959.

Uncle Zeke "CoolCat" was always a sharp dresser, as sharp as the toe of his shiny black cowboy boots, his fine black leather jackets, his gold imitation Rolex watches, his two carat cluster diamond rings, his Gucci belt, his diamond earring in one ear and his beautiful big white Afro. And also his collection of expensive leather hats.

He looked like classy old money. He had a beautiful big smile and a twinkle in his eyes. He always had some type of gift to give to everyone he came upon. Uncle Zeke was a good provider. He had a good job that paid well with Metro public works for more than thirty years and he had his side hustles. He and Aunt Frances raised seven boys in the house he bought, on seventh Avenue North, after their rented home, on Jo Johnson Street, burned down.

He would not let Aunt Frances work outside the home or allow her to learn to drive. Her job was to raise and take care of their boys. He made sure she had everything she needed to take care of them. He insisted that they attend Jackson Street Church of Christ where his name was on the roll, but he did not attend. It was the church that his sister and her family attended. Aunt Frances was raised up in the Primitive Baptist church. But she did what her husband wanted her to do.

He was very street smart, even when he was in his eighties people just could not get over on him. He loved cars and always had a fancy car and an old, restored Ford truck. No matter where he went, he was always packing. He taught his boys to always be prepared for whatever happens. Don't start nothing but be ready to protect yourself.

He had a collection of guns and knew how to use them. Uncle Zeke was always soft spoken and kind but everyone in the streets knew that he did not play. They knew not to mess with him or his family.

He enjoyed hunting, fishing and partying. He loved beautiful women and women loved him. Aunt Frances, his wife, was a very beautiful women but he messed around on her. Uncle Zeke was so handsome; he was thin and small framed; was very neat and always smelled good; he had high cheek bones, light green eyes, head full of soft, thick, curly straight hair and beautiful light caramel colored skin. He was always joking and laughing. He did not bother anyone, but you better not messed with him or his.

He lived alone, Aunt Frances had passed on, but his boys always checked on him. One day he was 85 years old, it was about three years after Aunt Frances had passed. A beautiful young lady knocked on Uncle Zeke's door. He was sitting on his green floral couch coved in plastic watching gun smoke on TV. He went to the door and asked, "who is it?" The young lady answer in a low soft voice, I'm Kaniya may I come in? He could see her through the curtains. She was thin, tall and very beautiful. He said smiling, come on in.

Kaniya came in and sat on the green floral sofa next to him. She sat there smiling at him. "You sure are handsome" she stated. He smiled looking in her eyes and asked her what do you want? She said I would like something to drink. He said I have Coke. She said, "it will be fine". He got the Coke for her. They were laughing and talking about the neighborhood changes. And he asked her again "why are you here. What do you want?"

He had a feeling that something was not right. She stated, "I would like to get to know you better cake daddy". He looked at her and said "girl, you are in your thirties, and I am in my eighties. What do you mean get to know me better?"

Before she could answer, there was another knock at the door. It was a young man named Abe. He pushed his way through the unlocked door and came into the front room. Abe asked Kaniya "what are you doing here?" Before she could answer, he looked at Uncle Zeke and said, "this is a robbery old man you better get me all of the money you got here". Uncle Zeke looked at him and took his time getting up. He was not afraid of him. "Move it, move it old man".

Uncle Zeke got up and said, "okay I have to get it". Abe said, "you better get it, or I am going to kick your old ass". He said, "I am so scared". The young man did not know who he was messing with. He must have been new in this area. Because everyone knows Zeke Marlow did not play.

Uncle Zeke told him "I got money and lots of it, but you have to give me time to get it". The Abe had a smile on his face, "a lot of it he thought". He could see dollar bills floating in his mind. Uncle Zeke walked into the bedroom to his solid Oak dresser with Abe and Kaniya standing there watching every move he made.

The young man was so greedy that he could smell all that money. He was thinking that he had hit the jackpot now. The man said "you better hurry up old man I am not playing with you. I don't have all day." Uncle Zeke said, "okay it is taking time because it is a lot of it". I got it, here it is" he stated.

Then he pulled both hands out of the drawer with two forty-five pistols shooting both at the same time. Bang, bang bang bang bang, bang bang. Hitting Abe in the right leg and left shoulder.

Abe yelled "all shit "and they ran as fast as they could dodging bullets, out of the door. Kaniya fell trying to get down the high steps. Abe yelled, "you better get your big ass down these steps before your get shot".

The neighbors who adored Uncle Zeke and saw them go in his home, heard the shots got his gun and run to see what was going on. Bob, the big six ft eight in. white neighbor who was a bouncer, pointed his pistol and yelled stop right there and retained both of them.

They called the police, while Uncle Zeke and the neighbor held them at gun point until the police arrived. By then other neighbors had showed up to help. Uncle Zeke is an expert shooter and could have killed bother of them if he wanted too but he just wanted to stop them.

When the police came, they ask Uncle Zeke if he shot the man. He said yes. The white male policeman told him he would have to go to jail without finding out what really happened.

They took him to jail and booked him an eighty-five-year-old black man. And took his gun and bullets. When he went before the night judge, he asked Uncle Zeke what he was charged with? He told him I was being robbed in my home and I shoot him. He asked, you shoot him in your home? uncle said yes. The judge asked to see the officer that charged him. He asked him why in the hell did he bring this man in. He shot the man in his home. What is wrong with you? Give him his gun and bullets back. Take this man back to his home and let him go. The robbers were taken to the hospital then to jail where they were persecuted. Uncle Zeke got his wings in 2019. The man and Kaniya were still in jail.

The man and Kaniya learned a big lesson that day. If you are going to rob, they should check out who they plan to rob before they do it. Everyone in the community knew that Zeke Marlow may be old, but he did not play. He is nice and friendly but don't cross him. He had more than money in his dresser.

Uncle Zeke learned not to let every pretty face in his house. Kaniya was just setting him up for her boyfriend to rob him. They all learned some mighty big life lessons.

MY FIRST RECOGNIZED ANSWERED PRAYER

The choir was really singing, the spirit was very high and people were jumping, dancing and shouting hallelujah, glory to His name, thank you Jesus. Mama raised us up in the spirited Clayton Ave Primitive Baptist Church. Daddy was a good man but did not go to church. Mama's parents Pop George and Annie Davis required her to bring the children up in church, they turn out much better in life when raised in the church, Pop George declared. All of her siblings where required by Pop George and Annie to raise their children up in church also. Even though they were all grown, out of respect for them, mama and her siblings always followed their parent's directions.

We did not have access to a car, Daddy had a car, but he did not take us to church. He rested on Sunday after working six long hard days a week, and there were few buses in our neighborhood. So, we walked on the sidewalk up 27th Ave and Clifton and 40th Ave north to church every Sunday with the little ones on our hips. Mama carried Brenda who was three years old, and I carried Debra who was barely two years. Rachel who was six years old walked on the sidewalk by mama's side. We sang songs" Mary had a little lamb, a little lamb, a little lamb" as we walked along. I never thought that there was any other way to go to church but sing and walk. Mama made it so much fun.

We wore pretty little ruffled dresses that mama made for us. In the winter when it was too cold to walk, daddy, the Pastor and other church members made sure that we had rides.

We sang in the Sunshine choir. Pretty, tall seventeen-year-old Tammy was the Sunshine choir director and pianist who played as we marched in singing. "We are marching to Zion, beautiful, beautiful Zion we are marching onward to Zion that beautiful city of God. We looked up to her and thought that she was something.

We also went to the children's Sunday school class where we learned about prayer, forgiveness and Christian living.

After the fun Sunday school class, we had to listen to balding, short, kindhearted Rev. Crumley, in his baggy Grey suit, preach his long-drawn-out sermon. I could see older men and women jumping up yelling preach Pastor and others shouting amend, come on now but I did not understand anything that he said.

Mr. and Mrs. Toliver, who were members lived next to the church. They had a little shop in a small white brick-o-block building between the church and their home. They sold penny candy, drinks and cookies to the neighborhood children. It was whispered that Mr. Toliver was also running numbers there to the adults.

Short plump quiet spirited Mrs. Toliver would often have Sunday dinner for us before we walked home about two miles away. She always served bitter tasting collard greens that she grew outside in the yard by her front door.

In Sunday school we learned about what prayer is and how to pray. The old gray headed slightly bent teacher, Mother Ransom, told us to ask God for whatever we wanted or needed. She stated God will give it to you if you believe He will. She had us practice in the class."

Oh Lord, almighty God, we praise your Holy name. Thank you for your son, Jesus. Please forgive us for our sins. Then ask the Lord Jesus for what you wanted. Thank you Lord in Jesus mighty name we pray Amen." I still use this prayer sometimes today.

I was about eight years old. Tall, skinny caramel colored with thick pretty hair. We were poor but did not know it. I thought that I did not have clothing like the other neighborhood kids because mama made our dresses, pants and shirts. Actually, she could sew better than the clothing in the stores, but I did not know it at the time. I asked God to give me a store-bought dress and a pair of shoes thinking that they would be better than what I had. I expected them to be a beautiful pink lace dress with black patent leather shoes like mama made for us but better.

The tall, dark chocolate colored, fifty-year-old greying lady that live next door to us, Mrs. Karen Fallberry, worked for the white folks. She was their maid and always brought home their children's old clothing that they no longer wanted. They were very expensive clothing. One day Mrs. Fallberry yelled out to mama "Free, Free I got something for you Free. Come over and have some chess pie with me" thirty-year-old Mama yelled back "yes ma-am." When mama came back home, she had a bag of white folks used clothing. Among other things, she sent a dress and a pair of shoes that fitted me. The dress was a lightly worn, plain long sleeve light brown, long wasted heavy cotton and the shoes were light and dark brown laced up brogans. They both were a perfect fit.

I thought to myself, "I don't want them ugly things. She is always bringing those white folk hand me down clothing to us." I could not say that to mama. A child stayed in a child's place in those days. I put them in my dresser drawer. Each child had their own drawer in the large old antique oakwood chest of drawers that mama's daddy Pop George built for her family.

I was use to beautiful little ruffled dresses that mama made and pretty expensive black patten leather shoes to match from the Goodwill twenty-five cent. My mama was very progressive and resourceful. She wanted her girls to always look good. She could buy much better things in the Goodwill than she could afford to buy in the retail stores. In those days, the donations to the Goodwill were very high quality gently used clothing. She took some of the money she saved and bought ribbon for our hair.

One day I was praying to our almighty God, "Father, Mother Ransom said to ask you for what we wanted, and you would give it to us. I asked you for a store-bought dress and shoes and you did not give them to me. I don't understand."

Our Father God said back to me, as clear as if He was standing in front of me, I sent you a store-bought dress and shoes and you did not want them. They were ugly, remember.

For the first time I realized that God did answer my prayer. I did not want what He gave me. But he did answer my prayer. That year the winter was very cold. The dress kept me warm, and the shoes protected my feet from lots of cold snow and wet rain.

The moral of this story is to first, recognize answered prayer. Ask God specifically for what you want and be grateful when He gives it to you. Even if it is not just what you asked for. He can see farther than you can see. Be grateful for whatever He gives you.

I have thus become a powerful intercessory prayer warrior. I recognize the answered prayer according to His divine Will and am so grateful for whatever He gives me and whomever I am praying for. Thank you, Jesus.

WORDS OF WISDOM

Thoughts of My Mother

Savannah Obera Davis Freeman 11/11/1925-3/26/2017

Beautiful, joyful, precious thoughts of her are locked in my heart to stay. The light in her eyes, the glow in her smile, her passion, her drive, her spunk. Her touch, her embrace, her smell of expensive Givenchy- Ysatis perfume; her matching hats, suites, shoes, purses and jewelry, when I think of these things it makes me laugh. How she could get a prayer through because of her strong beliefs and obedience to our Lord God. How she read the Bible three or four times all the way through in the last five years. When I think of these things and the overflowing love in her heart for her family, her church, friends and community, these are the thoughts that I hold on to, that help me carry on without her here.

Blessed, precious, memories of my mother, gets me through each day.

When she lived with me, we planted flowers, vegetable gardens, baked million-dollar pound cakes, made cornbread, yeast rolls and chicken and dressing casseroles. We made Mamannie's chow chow and cucumber pickle relish. We canned strawberry jam and apple jelly. We stitched quilts and grew African violets. And as I do all of these things that she taught me well, I know that she would be so proud of me now.

The exciting friendship we shared brings me comfort and lasting peace.

We could laugh and talk for hours. We like all of the same things. She told me old family secrets and stories. That Pop was very smart but too smart for his own breeches. He was a Deacon in the Primitive Baptist Church. She told me that sometimes Pop would run away from his home in Columbia, TN. He would come and stay with us. I remember it but did not know why he was there. She said he would tell her he was going to walk to the neighborhood diner and have a fish. She followed him one day and he was sitting at the table with a big bottle of beer. Deacons could not drink alcohol in public in those days. She said she felt that Pop did not like her. I said why do you think that?

He always comes to you when he runs away from home. We laughed out loud. She was so tickled. I know that she told me all of these things so that I could carry on once she was gone on. So, I think about all of her stories and stop crying and laugh, laugh, laugh....

When I am missing her presence God takes me in his big strong arms. God covers me with His Love, His Grace, and His Mercy. God's strength is my strength, His power and faithfulness will never fail me. When I am missing her presence, with God's touch, I will think of something funny about her and begin to laugh. I am comforted- Jesus said I will go away but I will send you a comforter, the Holy Spirit. The Holy Spirit turns my tears into joy. I am handling my grief- by the healing blood of Jesus which covers me. I am at peace; Jesus gives me peace that surpasses all understanding. Rest on in Paradise dear mother until we meet again.

2020 Mama's Legacy Notes

Savannah Obera Freeman

Reflections of her Legacy

Nickname - Mutt

Her favorite color -Green

Flower- African violets, cannons, zinnias, petunias, roses and Mums.

Things that are Important to her- her family her church and her friends

Her crafts- quilting, cooking and baking, garden, making jams jellies chow chow and relishes.

Favorite things to bake- Pound cakes, caramel cake, carrot cakes, Mamannie's egg pie, potato yeast rolls and cookies.

Things that she enjoyed - Sunday dinners.

Things that she loved- teaching her children and grandchildren how to cook and bake. Working in her garden. Reading her bible and quilting.

Church hats, good perfume, beautiful jewelry shoes and stockings that matched her outfit, going to quilting conferences, her dolls.

Songs that she sang-use me in your service. Draw me nearer everyday. I am willing to run all of the way.

Favorite China- Franciscan desert rose.

Her favorite scripture-Ps 119

Things that she was very strict about- going to church.

Favorite places to go- visit her family, going to church, antiquing and junk store shopping Cracker Barrel, TJMAXX and Macy's also visiting the cemetery.

GOD'S AMAZING GRACE

King David wrote about the cross, prophesying the coming of the Messiah, a signal of the devil's loss. A young virgin gave birth to the Savior of the world, He was born in Bethlehem of Judea, His birthplace foretold. How on earth were the shepherds chosen to hear the Angels sing, or the wisemen from the east directed to the newborn King?

The young boy Jesus found in the Temple Court, listening and talking to the teachers with the spirit of the Lord upon Him. How in the world did John the Baptist speak of Him, water turn to wine, the sea obeyed, and the nets were filled Five thousand fed with five fish and two loaves? How?

How is it that the blind could see, the lame could walk, the deaf could hear, the mute could talk, the leper saw his hands made clean and Lazarus arose at His command. How?

The disciples fled on that fateful night only to die convinced that Jesus was right. His chosen people turn on Him and let a ruthless killer free, as they scourged the Holy One. He forgave His tormentors as He hung upon the cross, He died so that we could have eternal life. The veil was torn, the stone rolled away. He spoke so assuredly that He would rise in three days.

What did it mean? How could it be? It is God's amazing love for us, that we will have eternal life if we only believe.

Inspired by a similar poem found on the internet by anonymous.

DON'T GRIEVE FOR ME

Don't Grieve for me. Aunt Helen Belafonte Davis passed during the covid pandemic. If our loved ones, that have passed on, could speak to us now, I believe that we would hear them say "Don't grieve for me, for God has given me peace." When I heard Him call, I stepped out of this body, took His hand and left my earthly presence.

I am now in the presence of the Lord. No more discomfort, no more sorrows, no more suffering for me. God has me now and I am rejoicing with the angels and with my loved ones surrounding me. So, please focus on my gain and not your loss, for God has me now. I am at peace.

I fought the good fight, I kept the faith and heard the Lord say to me, Come on in my good and faithful servant. God has me now, I am on the other side of the pearly gates, praising and worshiping at His feet. I put on my robe and tell the story of how I made it over. God has me now. I am at peace.

Carry on my traditions and create some of your own. Share my pictures and stories with my loved ones and new family members to come. I know that you will miss me. However, I will always be with you, just think about me and you will feel my presence in your heart. We will meet again, when it is time, on this side of Jordan. God has me now I am at peace.

In honor of Aunt Helen's passing

A TRIBUTE TO MY SISTER COUSIN

Laura Belle Davis Mitchell how do
I love you sister cousin, let me count the ways.

I love your vast accumulation of knowledge and understanding of the Word of God and your spiritual wisdom, interpretation, commentary and life application of the Word of God.

I love the way you go through a severe life storm with your helmet of salvation on, shield of faith in place and spiritual umbrella up protecting yourself against the heavy sheets of rain and damaging wind, coming out of the storm completely dry. Not even one drop of water of damage could be found.

I love that you can be put in life's fiery, extremely hot furnace of trials and tribulations and come out whole, not even smelling like smoke. You are a spirit filled awesome woman of God.

I love how you can deliver a sermon that will make the world stand up straight and declare what shall I do to be saved? How you can pray a prayer that will make them jump up and shout praises to the Lord Jesus Christ, our Savior. Your prayers make my hair stand up on my bald head. I am so proud to be your family member.

I love it when you start something, whatever the project, you never give up until you have reached your goal and your project has been completed, no matter what the outcome.

104

I love it when you say as we are planning family events, and I am concerned that family will not want to come, you assure me that, "whoever comes will and whoever don't want but the show will still go on. Even if there is no one there but me and you". Then you take it to God in prayer. It always turns out the way it is supposed to turn out.

You were born just a few months before me, and I know that we were together on the other side. I think that you are so beautiful inside and out. You are my idol. I love the thought of who you are, Wise Woman, Seasoned Spirit, Godly Soul, loving, kind with a forgiving heart and much much more.

I will always love you, my sister cousin. Reverend mother Laura Mitchell.

Your Cousin,
Anne Buchanan

Rev. Laura Mitchell is the first-born child of Ida Bruce Davis Frierson my mother Savannah Obera Davis Freeman's older sister. They were best friends.

SEASONED QUEEN

I am a seasoned senior Queen; I wonder just what has flavored my life so well that it makes my seasoning so great? Let's take a look into me. Is it my home? – which is my haven, filled with the spirit of the Lord, beautiful, clean; rich with colors, the sounds of soothing music and smells of delicious food cooking. Full of happiness and Joy inside it's many walls? Where negativity, drama, stresses of this world are absolutely not allowed here.

Is it my beauty? The wrinkles in my skin, the white in my hair, my belly from giving so many births shakes like jelly when I laugh; the extra junk in my truck, or my boobs that are big and soft just perfect for a infants snuggle; is it the shine in my eyes, the light in my smile or the dance in my step when I walk.

Is it my food? My crispy fried chicken, blackened catfish, fresh turnip greens on my stove, baked corn bread, sweet chess pies or my three-layer caramel cakes?

Is it my maturity- the lines under my beautiful eyes, around my voluptuous lips or down my long neck. Or is it my light that shines so bright from the depths of my soul because I have made it through so many of life's ups and downs.

Is it my wisdom? so many life's lessons learned good and bad, by overcoming so many spiritual storms that comes bearing gifts or life changing experiences that strengthened my knowledge base, or is it my intense research of so many interesting world subjects politics religions and science etc.; or my love for studying family history getting to know ancestors that have passed on?

Is it my inner mystery? which makes me hold my head up high, My love for the Lord Jesus, my strong Christian faith, my work in the church or the love in my heart for so many family members alive or dead. Or is it because of having so many amazing, good friends and acquaintances?

I think that I am a Seasoned Queen because of everything that I have experienced in this life. I am a seasoned Queen not an old lady, but seasoned and I am so very proud of my life.

GOD'S SUPER MARKET

While driving up life's interstate in my brand new red convertible Mercedes, on a beautiful Saturday morning in the fall of 2008. I passed a big flashing billboard sign that said God's Super Market, exit to the right. Very curious about this market, I decided to check it out. I wondered what kind of marvelous things I would find inside. I pulled on to the parking lot and found a parking place, near the front door, with my name on it, not sure if that spot was for me. I parked my car there carefully.

The next thing I knew, I was standing inside the most amazing Super Market that I have ever seen. There were legends of Angels as far as I could see. Angels in the front of the store, the back, in the isles, Angels everywhere. One of them gave me a shopping cart and said shop very carefully my dear. Everything a Believer could ever need was in the store that day.

Added several packs of Salvation to my basket. Instructions on how to be saved from eternal separation from God, something that I would surely need. Put a big bag of Faith in my basket. Belief and trust in God are really needed in this world today. I added two one-gallon cans of Grace. Unmerited blessings and favor, from God, will go a long way for believers and unbelievers as well. I also added two extra-large bottles of Mercy-God's undeserved forgiveness from sin.

I came upon Praise and Worship and giving honor to God, which was on the lower shelf, so I put some in my cart as well. I saw that Endurance, Strength and Courage were on the next shelf, so I took all that I could fit. Understanding, patience, love and peace were around the corner on the top shelve so I added them to my basket as well. Let us not forget fellowship and stewardship. I was like a child in a candy store. I had to get them also.

Wisdom, knowledge and experience was on the next aisle, and I could not leave without adding some of each to the top of the cart. I started to the self-checkout counter to pay. I thought I had everything I needed to fulfill the Lord's divine Will for me. As I started to check out, I saw joy and happiness. I just had to take some of them, so I carried them in my hand. I scanned all of my items but there were no prices to be found. I asked the Angel at customer service, "Where are the prices? I need to know how much I have to pay?"

The nice Angel said to me with a glow on her face, there is no charge my child, just take them everywhere you go. I ask again, do you mean I don't have to pay anything? And she said, Jesus paid your bill, on the old rugged cross at Calvert 2000 years ago. Now, take them. Use them everywhere you go to spread the good News of our Lord and Savior Jesus Christ. The Lord be with you, my child.

This story was inspired by Heaven's Grocery Store found on social media. Author Unknown

The moral of the story, take the gifts and tools that Jesus has for you and use them to evangelize the lost and bring glory to His name.

CORPORATE PRAYER

Over Our Family, Friends and Enemies

Our Father Oh God. How excellent is your holy name in all the universe

Oh God how we thank you for your Son Jesus and the opportunity to be saved from eternal separation from you, oh God.

Lord we have all sinned and fallen short of the glory of God. We come before you with repentant hearts and we ask you for forgiveness for our sins known and unknown.

Father, Oh God, we thank you for the blessings of healing in our bodies, our minds and our hearts. That we might have peace that is beyond all our understanding.

We thank you that every attack of the enemy on our lives is disarmed in the name of Jesus. That no weapon formed against us shall prosper and that every tongue that rises up against us shall be put to shame in Jesus mighty name.

We thank you that every plan of the enemy for our lives be dissolved and that you place your Hedge of Protection around us, in the name and power of Jesus.

We thank you that you knew what you had planned for us before you placed us in our mother womb.

We thank you that You are all powerful, all knowing and all seeing and the devil does not have the final say in any battle or situation that we go through.

We thank you that you have prepare a table before us in the presence of our enemy. You anoint our heads with oil and our cups runs over.

I thank you that, because of you, we are the head and not the tail. In Jesus name.

Order our steps, Father that our lives will bring glory to your name and we
will hear you say well done my good and faithfully servant.

Father, we give your name all the glory, honor and praise in the name above all names. The name of Jesus.
Amen and amen.

LET'S EAT!
FAMILY RECIPES

Ann's Peach dump cake cobbler

(1) 28 oz can Delmonti peaches

1 Tbs lemon juice

1 Tbs sugar

1/8 tsp vanilla

1 Tbs Jack Daniels

1 rolled pie crust

1/2 Duncan Heinz cake mix

1 tsp cinnamon

1 tsp nutmeg

1 stick butter

1/2 cup buttermilk

1 Tbs sugar

*Line 9x9 pan with pie crust

*Add peaches, Jack Daniels, spice, flavoring and lemon juice to peaches

*Cover peaches with cake mix.

*Melt butter and mix with buttermilk pour over cake mix.

*Sprinkle Tbs sugar

*Bake 350F for one hour until Golden brown and set

Ann's Pound Cake

*All ingredients room temp

*Grease pan, flour then spray with Baker's Joy.

4 cups flour, 1 tsp baking powder, pack lemon pudding, tsp salt and 1 tsp nutmeg.

3 cups sugar

4 sticks butter

6 eggs

1/4 cup butter milk

1 Tbs vanilla, 2 tsp lemon extract and 1/2 tsp butter extract.

*Cream butter and sugar for 7 minutes.

*Add 1 egg at the time

*Add flavoring extracts.

*Add flour mixture alternating with milk. Beat just until completely mixed.

*Bake 350 1 hour 15 mins until golden brown top is risen and set. I use a cake tester.

Ann's fudge pie

*Heat oven to 350F

*One deep dish pie crust in pan. Place it on a glass pie plate or cookie sheet.

1 1/4 white 1/4 dark brown

1 stick butter

1/4 C flour

1/2 tsp salt

6 Tbs premium cocoa

1/2 C semi-sweet chocolate chips

1/4 C cream

3 large eggs beaten

Tbs vanilla

Pie crust

*Melt butter cocoa and chocolate chips

*Add sugar, flour, and salt, add one egg at the time

*Add cream and vanilla.

*Bake about 1 hour until the top is raised and set

Easy Buttermilk pie

Heat oven to 350F

Store bought pie crust

<u>Makes one pie</u>

1 stick butter

1 cup sugar

1/4 cup flour

1/4tsp salt

3 eggs

1 cup whole buttermilk

2 tsp pure vanilla extract

1 tsp almond extract

1/2 lemon extract

*All ingredients must be at room temperature.

*Melt butter in microwave, add sugar, salt and flour. Mix with a whisk.

*Beat in one egg at a time

*Add flavorings

*Mix in buttermilk

*Pour into pie crust.

*Set on a cookie sheet

*Bake on bottom rack of oven about 1 hour until the top is golden brown and rises up and is set.

*Best if bake the day before you need it.

Easy Fudge Pound Cake

*Bake in tub or large Bundt pan.

*Heat oven 350F

*All ingredients room temperature

Box brownie mix

Box fudge cake mix

1 tsp baking powder

1 Cup dark brown sugar

Box instant chocolate pudding mix

4 Tbs cocoa

8 oz cream cheese

1 cup cooking oil

4 extra large eggs

1 cup full fat butter milk

1 Tbs premium vanilla

*Mix all ingredients in a heavy-duty mixture for about 5 mins.

*Bake 1 hour until the center rises. I use a cake tester. Let it cool in the pan for 20 minutes. Turn out and let cool completely.

*Cover with chocolate glaze.

Sweet potato Chess pie

1 pie crust. (I use Kroger frozen deep dish). Or 1 Kroger pre-made rolled pie crust from the cooler section. Or make one from scratch.

*Heat oven to 375°F

*Important. Eggs, butter, sweet potatoes and cream must be room temperature.

1 1/2 C sugar

1 stick butter

1 Tbs all purpose (plain)flour

1/4 tsp salt

1 heaping tsp nutmeg

1/4 cinnamon

Pinch of ground cloves and ginger (optional)

1 tsp premium vanilla extract

1Tbs lemon juice

1 1/2 cup mashed sweet potatoes (I use baked organic potatoes)

3 extra large eggs

2 Tbs cream

2 Tbs Jack Daniels (optional) (alcohol bakes out)

*In a large bowl, melt butter until it is hot in the microwave. Add sugar, flour, salt, spice.

*Add lemon juice to mashed sweet potatoes mix well, then add them to the sugar mixture.

*Using a whisk, mix sweet potato and sugar, butter mixture well. Whisk in room temp eggs one at a time. Add vanilla, Jack Daniels and cream. Whisk until well mixed and pour into pie shell.

123

*Place pies on a cookie sheet on the lower rack. Bake until Golden brown, the center rises up and is firm to touch. About 50 mins to an hour.

*Let completely cool. Better if baked the day before you serve it.

*Serve with cool whip or ice cream.

Mamannie's Sweet Potato Meringue pie recipe.

I rewrote this because I cannot get to the originals at this time.

Mama told me that Mamannie used her 150-year-old egg pie recipe and added sweet potatoes. Dropped the lemon extract and added nutmeg.

This is the recipe that mama used most of the time. She made sweet potato chess for people that did not like meringue.

Crust

1 deep dish pie crust.

*I use frozen Kroger brand.

*Mamannie made her crust from Scratch. I do not have her crust recipe.

Heat oven to 350°F

3 extra large egg yolks (save whites for meringue. Do not refrigerate).

1 1/2 cup sugar

2 Tbs flour

1/4 tsp salt

1 heaping tsp ground nutmeg

1/2 stick butter soft

1/2 cup cream (May use fresh whole or canned milk)

1 tsp premium vanilla

1 Tbs lemon juice

1 1/2 cups mashed sweet potato.

(I use baked organic sweet potatoes).

*Beat egg yolks until thick and yellow

(like whipped cream) for about 3-5 minutes. (Use a hand mixer if just making 1 pie, may not be enough yolks for a stand mixer to beat properly. I use a stand mixer because I always make 2 or more pies).

*Slowly add sugar, flour, salt and nutmeg. Add lemon juice to potatoes then beat in sweet potatoes to egg mixture. Add soft butter then cream and vanilla.

*Pour into crust. Bake on lower rack of oven until brown, center is risen, set and firm to touch. About 45 minutes to 1 hour. Be sure the center is risen, firm and set before removing from the oven.

*Remove from oven. Turn oven up to 450°F. To bake meringue.

Meringue.

This is my recipe. I do not have Mamannie's recipe. I will check with some of the cousins to see if anyone has it.

Egg whites room temp.

2 Tbs sugar per egg white

1 Tbs corn starch for 3 egg whites

1/4 tsp salt

1/2 tsp premium vanilla

Beat egg whites until soft peak forms.

Beat in sugar, corn starch and salt slowly. Beat until stiff peaks form. Add vanilla.

(I mix sugar, corn starch and salt together). Then spoon in slowly.

Cover pie with meringue covering all edges of the pie.

Bake until light golden brown. Watch closely.

Remove from oven and let cool completely for about 2 or more hours. Best to bake early in the morning and to serve in the evening. Best the next day.

If first you don't succeed, practice makes perfect.

Southern Chess Pie

6 eggs beaten

3 cups sugar

1 stick butter

2 Tbs corn meal

1 Tbs flour

1/2 tsp salt

1 Tbs vanilla

1/2 tsp lemon extract

1 tsp vinegar

4 Tbs cream

2 deep dish pie crust

*Melt butter, add sugar, stir with a spoon, and dry ingredients. Add wet ingredients mix well with a whisk pour into 2 pie crust.

*Bake on 350°F about an hour until the top rises up and pies are dark and golden. Pies are best when made the day before serving.

DeeDee's gooey bars

*Preheat oven to 350°F

*Spray an 8x10 glass baking dish with oil. I use Baker's Joy

*Crust

Box yellow cake mix

1 stick butter

1 large egg

1 tsp vanilla

Top layer

8 oz cream cheese

2 eggs

1 stick butter room temp

1/2 tsp salt

1 tsp vanilla extract

4 cups powdered sugar

*Mix cake mix, butter, egg and vanilla in a stand mixer and press into an 8x10 prepared glass baking dish.

*In the same mixing bowl, mix cream cheese, butter, vanilla, salt and powdered sugar. Pour over the crust.

*Bake until golden brown, rises in the middle and is set. Let it cool completely then refrigerate for 2 hours.

*Cut in squares and enjoy.

Ann's Carrot cake bars

*Crust

2 boxes cake mix

2 cups finely grated carrots

1 cup chopped pecans

2 eggs and 2 sticks butter

1 tsp ground cinnamon

1/2 tsp. Nutmeg, Allspice

Ginger and cloves

2 tsp vanilla

Cream cheese topping

8 on cream cheese

4 cups powdered sugar

2 Tbs flour

½ tsp salt

1 Tbs lemon juice and lemon zest

2 eggs

1 tsp vanilla extract

2 Tbs butter

Spray 9x13 pan, line pan with parchment paper and spray the paper.

Mix crust ingredients and press into pan.

Mix topping ingredients with a mixer. Pour over the crust.

Bake for about 1 hour until golden brown and set firm.

Gooey Butter Cookies

Cake mix (I use Duncan Hines yellow cake mix)

Cream cheese

1 Stick of butter

1 egg

2 tsp Vanilla extract

1/2 tsp Lemon extract

Powdered

*Mix all ingredients, refrigerator 30 minutes. Roll into balls.

*Roll balls in powdered sugar. Bake in preheated oven to 350F on a cookie sheet with parchment paper.

*Add nuts or anything that you want to add.

Tracye's Vanilla Almond Tea Cakes

2 cups flour

2 Tbs vanilla instant pudding

3/4 tsp salt

3/4 cup sugar

1 cup soft butter room temp.

2 tsp vanilla

1tsp almond extract

Best sugar and butter until creamy and light add vanilla and almond extracts.

Mix instant pudding and salt in flour.

Add mix with sugar mixture.

Scoop into balls and flatten on. Cookie sheet.

Bake 10 mins 350F until very light brown.

Mamannie's Tea Cakes

*Heat oven to 350F

4 cups flour

1 tsp baking powder

1 tsp soda

1/4 tsp salt

2 cups sugar

1cup shortening

1 cup sour cream

3 eggs

1 tsp Vanilla

Sift dry ingredients together. Mix like biscuits. Cut shortening in. Add eggs, vanilla and sour cream. Roll out and cut thin with biscuit cutter. Bake for 10 minutes. Let cool. Enjoy.

Ann's Tomato Soup Cake

*Heat oven to 350F

*Oil and flour tube pan. (I use baker's joy)

3 cups self-rising flour

1 cup raisin

1 cup chopped pecans

1 tsp cinnamon,

1 Tbs allspice,

1 Tbs nutmeg

1-2 tsp ginger

1/2 tsp clove

1 Tbs vanilla

1 cup oil

2 cup sugar

1 can tomato soup

4 eggs

*Mix oil, eggs, soup, vanilla and sugar in a heavy-duty mixer.

*In a large bowl, mix dry ingredients, spice, pecans and raisins and add to the wet ingredients. Pour in tube pan and bake 50 minutes to 1 hour until the top rises up and sets, I use a cake tester.

*Let cool for 10 minutes then remove from pan. Let cool. Add powder sugar glaze.

*1 cup powdered sugar, pinch salt, 1Tbs melted butter, 1/4 tsp vanilla and 1Tbs lemon juice. Mix and pour over cake. Let dry. Taste best next day.

Mamannie's 150-year-old recipe

Egg pie enlarged filling to 1 1/2 size.

1 deep dish pie crust

*Heat oven to 350F

*I set the frozen pie crust and aluminum pan in a Pyrex or ceramic pie plate to bake. They conduct heat better. Or set the pies on a cookie sheet.

*Mama said bake on the lower rack of the oven. With today's new ovens you may not need to use the lower rack. Mamannie used a wood stove until they moved to town.

*Mama also told me that Mamannie made her pies in a 12in. black cast iron skillet. So, she must have qua-tripled the recipe for one pie. She made 2 pies so her family of 12 could have 2 servings each.

4 jumbo egg yolks or five large.

1 1/2 cups sugar

3 Tbs flour

1/2 tsp salt

3/4 stick buttery

3/4 cup cream

2 tsp premium Vanilla extract

1/8 tsp Watkins lemon extract

Sometimes I add 1/4 tsp nutmeg(optional).

*Beat egg yolks until thick and yellow about 3-5 minutes. It will get thick like whipped cream. Slowly add sugar, then flour and salt while beating. Add soft butter. Then add cream and flavoring. Pour into pie crust.

*(I mix sugar, flour and salt together then add slowly). Mama would never do that. She said we should always stick to the original recipe.

*Bake until dark brown, the center is risen and set firm to touch. Remove from oven and increase the temp to 450F to bake the meringue.

*The pie texture will not come out right if it is not baked long enough. Be sure the center is firm, and the color is rich brown iced tea color brown.

Chocolate Fudge Cake

Preheat oven to 350°F

Prepare a stem /bundt pan with oil and flour. I use Baker's Joy. Stem pan does not have ridges.

2 sticks room temperature butter

2 cups sugar

4 large eggs

2 cups White Lilly flour

1/2 tsp salt

1 tsp baking powder

1 box instant chocolate pudding

1/2 cup cocoa

1 cup buttermilk

1 Tablespoon Vanilla extract

*Cream butter and sugar for 4 minutes in a heavy mixer. Add 1 egg at a time. Add vanilla.

*Mix all dry ingredients together in a separate bowl. Add to wet ingredients alternating with butter and milk. Pour in the pan and bake for about 1 hour or until the top rises and is set.

*Let cool completely.

Chocolate glacé

1 cup powdered sugar

1-2 Tbs cocoa

Pinch of salt

Tbs soft butter

1/2 tsp vanilla

- 1 tsp milk +extra until you can pour the thick glacé over the cake.

Mix and glace the cake.

Christmas Fruitcake

For the Cake:

2 Cups Butter

2 Cups packed brown sugar

6 Large eggs

2tsp Apple pie spice

2 2/3 Cup self-rising flour

½ Cup grapejuice

3Tbsp Vanilla Extract

3 ½ Cups candied fruit

10oz Chopped dates

4 Cups chopped pecans

*Read the entire recipe before beginning. Do not preheat the oven!

*In a mixer mix the butter and sugar until fluffy. Add eggs one at a time, beating in between. Add Apple pie spice and vanilla extract. Add grape juice and mix well.

*Add flour and beat for 2 minutes on medium speed. In a separate bowl add 1/3 CUP FLOUR then add your fruit and mix until fruit is coated well with flour. Add pecans and dates and mix well. Pour batter into bowl with fruit and nuts. Mix well.

*Spray pans with baking spray and fill 3/4 full of batter. Put cake in a cold oven and then put on Bake at 300 degrees and bake 30 minutes. Turn oven down to 250 degrees and bake for 2 hours.

Continues on next page >>>>>>>

For pecan and fruit topping on the cake:

Jelly or marmalade (8oz)

1-2 Cups of large mixed colored candied fruits (Your choice. I like red and green cherries.

4 Cups of whole pecans

*Heat jelly (your choice apple or orange marmalade) in a non-stick small pot or skillet. Pour over fruit and mix until fruit and nuts are coated well.

My choice of fruits:

1 Cup Fruit and peel old English mix or extra fancy (these are chopped small)

1 Cup Tropical Mix

1 Cup mixed pineapple and cherries (half these) (10oz)

Chopped dates

TIP: WHEN YOU BUY FRUIT AND NUTS GET PLENTY FOR TOP OF CAKES TOO!

Microwave Chocolate Pie

1 (9 inch) pie shell, baked

1 cup white sugar

¼ cup cornstarch

½ cup unsweetened cocoa powder

¼ teaspoon salt

2 cups milk

3 egg yolks, beaten

1 stick butter,

1 teaspoon vanilla extract

3 egg whites, beaten

¼ teaspoon cream of tartar

6 tablespoons white sugar

½ teaspoon vanilla extract

*Preheat oven to 375 degrees F (190 degrees C).

*In a 1- and 1/2-quart casserole dish, mix together sugar, cornstarch, cocoa, salt and 1/2 cup of milk until smooth. Once it is mixed well, stir in remaining milk.

*Microwave on high for 5 to 8 minutes or until thick; stir halfway through cooking time.

*In a small bowl beat egg yolks. Temper egg yolks by adding a little bit of hot mixture, place a small amount of the hot mixture into the egg yolks and beat together. Stir back into original mixture in casserole dish. Microwave on high for 1 1/2 to 2 minutes or until thickened; stir frequently. Blend in butter and the 1 teaspoon of vanilla. Pour mixture into pastry shell.

To Make Meringue: In a small bowl, beat egg whites and cream of tartar until foamy. Gradually whip in 2 tablespoons of sugar at a time until stiff peaks form; stir in vanilla. Spread meringue over top of pie filling.

*Bake in preheated oven for about 8 minutes or just until meringue gets browned.

Citrus Pound Cake

*3 Cups sugar +zest of a large orange and large Lemon mixed in sugar. Let set for 24 hrs.

*Beat 3 sticks butter and 8 oz cream cheese for 1 minute in a heavy duty stand mixer with a whisk attachment.

*Add the 3 cups of sugar with citrus zest and beat for 10 minutes.

*Add 6 eggs 1 at a time.

*Add 1 Tbs vanilla extract, 1 tsp lemon extract.

3 Cups White Lilly plain flour

1 box Jello instant vanilla pudding

1 tsp baking powder

1/2 tsp salt.

*Mix all together.

1/4 cup heavy cream

1/4 cup sour cream

*Add flour alternating with the creams until no flour is showing.

*Bake in 12 c prepared with oil and floured stem pan.

*Bake 325F 1 hr. 20 minutes.

*Put a cup of water in the oven with the baking cake.

Pecan Pie

*All ingredients must be at room temperature.

*Bake 350°F in oven on bottom rack.

1 Cup dark brown sugar

1 Cup light corn syrup

1/2 stick butter melted

3 eggs

1/4 tsp salt

1 tsp vanilla

1 1/2 C roasted pecan halves

*Place in warm oven 300°F for 10 minutes

*Mix with a whisk butter, sugar, salt and syrup until smooth and creamy. Add eggs one at a time. Add vanilla then fold in pecans. Pour in crust and bake until center rises and is firm to touch. Let cool completely. Best served the next day.

Mamannie's Black Berry Cobbler.

Mamannie grew her blackberries in the garden. She picked the berries, cooked most of them so they could last in the winter.

She would save a gallon of the blackberries to make cobbler for dinner which was lunch time for us today. She used two twelve black cast iron skillets. She made the crust from lard and flour. Rolled it out and placed half of it in each skillet. She would cook the berries with butter and sugar on a wood burning stove.

She poured half in each skillet the

Put half in each skillet. She rolled out the other crust and covered the pies then baked them in the oven for about an hour until they were rich brown.

The updated recipes for the younger generation.

Two bags of frozen black berries about a pound or so.

1 box of butter flavored cake mix.

2 sticks butter melted plus 2 TBS cream or milk (cream optional)

1/2 cup sugar. Or more per taste.

1 Tbs lemon juice.

*Spray a glass baking dish with oil like Pam. Add the berries. Pour the lemon juice and sugar over the berries. Pour the dry cake mix over the berries.

*Pour the butter cream mixture over the cake mix.

*Bake in 350F oven until the top is rice brown. Let cool. Better the next day.

Chocolate Chip Cookies

*Heat oven to 350F

I use a lined cookie sheet.

2 sticks butter

1 cup brown sugar

1 cup white sugar

2 eggs

2 cups self-rising sugar

1 box vanilla instant pudding

1 cup old fashion oatmeal

1tsp vanilla extract

1 bag semi-sweet chocolate chips

*Cream butter and sugar, add one egg one at a time beat well. Add vanilla extract. Fold chips into flour. Add flour and pudding. Mix well.

*Bake on cookie sheet for about 10 minutes or until light to golden brown.

Chocolate Chip cookie remix

1 box butter flavored cake mix

1 box instant villa pudding

1/2 cup cooking oil

2 eggs

1/4 cup dark brown sugar

1/4 cup flour

2 tsp vanilla extract

1 bag semi-sweet chocolate chips

1 cup pecans optional

*Mix all dry ingredients together in a stand mixer enclosing chips and pecans.

*Mix all wet ingredients with dry and stir until moist.

*Form cookies into balls I use an ice cream scoop.

*Bake on a cookie sheet until light brown or golden brown if you like the crisp.

*Let cool on a cookie rack.

Pat's Sweet potato pound cake

1.5 cups mashed sweet potatoes

1.5 cups butter (soft)

2.5 cups light brown sugar (I do half white half brown)

6 large eggs

1 tablespoon nutmeg

I tablespoon cinnamon

1 tablespoon vanilla

1 teaspoon baking powder

Teaspoon salt

3 cups plain flour

*Cream butter and sugar 5 minutes until fluffy. Beat in eggs one at a time.

*Beat in cooled sweet potatoes. Add vanilla then all dry ingredients, adding flour little at a time. Beat about 20 seconds until smooth. Bake at 325 degrees for about 75 minutes in greased and floured pan until done.

*Let cool before turning out of pan Best when served the next day.

Mamannie's Egg Pie

Mamannie Davis 1896-1989 was my grandmother. This recipe that she passed on is over 150 years old. Read the recipe before starting. She says you must have the gift to make it right. Be sure to beat the egg yolks until thick and lemon yellow (about 3-5 minutes) and bake until the top is dark brown, it rises up in the center and is solidly set when gently touched. Mamannie said you have to have the gift to make this.

Heat oven to 375

One reg pie crust (I use Kroger brand.)

3 eggs separated

1 Cup sugar

2 Tbs flour

1/4 tsp salt

1/2 Stick soft butter

1/2 Cup cream or milk

2 tsp good quality vanilla

1/4 tsp lemon extract

Directions

*3 egg yolks beat until think and lemons yellow. About 4 minutes. I use jumbo eggs.

* Add 1 cup sugar. Use premium sugar.

Dry ingredients

2 Tbs flour

1/2 tsp salt

*Add the dry ingredients to eggs mixture slowly one at a time. beat until mixed well. Add 1 Tbs vanilla and 1/4 tsp lemon extract.

*Add 1/2 cup cream and 1/2 stick of very soft butter. The recipe calls for milk. I use cream, it comes out better. Beat until blended well.

*Be sure the egg yolks, butter and cream are at room temperature.

*Pour into pie crust. Bake 375 on the lower rack for about one hour until the top is dark brown, rises up in the middle and is set.

*Add meringue bake till golden brown. Best next day.

You may use any meringue recipe. This is the one that I use.

Meringue

*Beat 3 egg whites (room temperature) until peaks form. Mix 1 Tbs cornstarch and 1/4 tsp salt to 6 Tbs sugar. Add sugar mixture one Tbs at a time. Beat

Ann's old fashion yellow cake recipe.

*Heat oven to 350F

Butter, eggs and milk should be at room temperature.

Mama taught us to use White Lilly self-rising flour only. It is southern soft wheat flour.

I spray the cake pans with Baker's Joy.

*Remove the cake from the oven and place on an elevated surface so that air can flow around it. Let cool for 10 minutes before removing from the pan. Let cool completely before frosting.

1 cup butter

2 cups sugar

3 cups self-rising flour

1/2 tsp salt

1 tsp baking soda

1/2 tsp nutmeg (it is a very old flavor that will give a delicious mild warm flavor with the vanilla)

1 box instant pudding

4 eggs

1 cup milk (I like whole buttermilk)

1 Tbs vanilla extract

1 tsp lemon

*Cream room temperature butter, sugar and pudding until fluffy.

*Add room temperature eggs one at a time. Add flavoring.

*Mix and add dry ingredients alternating with room temperature milk until completely mixed. Do not over beat.

*Bake at 350F about 33 minutes. For layers about 45 minutes in tube pan until the top of the cake is set and the sides pull away from the pan. Put a toothpick in and when it comes out clean it is done.

Ann's Crunchy French Toast

Dry ingredients

1 Tbs panko breadcrumbs

1cup crushed cornflakes

1Tbs sugar

1 tsp flour

1/2 tsp nutmeg

1/4 tsp cinnamon

1Tbs butter

*Mix well

Wet ingredients

2 eggs beaten

2 Tbs heavy cream

1 Tbs sugar

1tsp flour

1/2 baking powder

1/8 tsp salt

1/4 tsp nutmeg

1/8 tsp cinnamon

1/4 tsp vanilla extract

4 small pieces of bread.

*Mix the custard mixture and soak the bread in it, both sides.

*Then press the soaked bread on both sides in to crust mixture.

*Add 1 Tbs olive oil and melt butter in a warm skillet. Put the toast in the very warm skillet. Brown on both sides. Have over on 450F. Put toast in the oven. Bake on one side then turn over and bake on the other side. Should be very crisp. plate and add a little pancake syrup. Enjoy.

Old Fashion Peanut Brittle

1/2 Cup of water

1 Cup white container syrup

2 Cup raw peanuts

Butter

3 Cup white sugar

2 tsp Vanilla

2 tsp baking soda

1/2 tsp salt

*Butter your cookie sheet

*Have all the ingredients ready. Measure all ingredients before starting.

*Timing is everything. Use a large, deep, heavy pot. Heat on medium heat.

*Need candy thermometer and timer.

*Pour sugar, syrup and water in the pot. Cook until 230F and water cooks out.

*Pour raw peanuts in. Sugar will slightly change color to light brown.

*Cook to 320- 310? Degrees.

*Add in Butter, soda and vanilla in fast while foaming. Mix then pour onto the cookie sheet. Let cool to touch about 1 hour. Break into pieces.

*You May use pecans or coconut or both.

Prune Cake

Aunt Willie Mae's and mama's (Savannah Obera) recipe. Aunt Willie Mae baked a prune cake for every family gathering. My mother baked the cake for one of her son-n-laws and for some family gatherings. Now that mama has passed on, I am teaching my daughter to make this cake.

2 cups of self-rising flour. (I use White Lilly + 1/2 tsp baking soda.

1 Tbs cinnamon, 1 tsp allspice, 1 tsp ginger, 1/2 tsp clove.

1 white sugar 1 cup dark brown sugar

1 cup canola oil

3 X-large eggs

2 Cups chopped prunes soak in 1/2 cup boiling water drained then add 4 Tbs Rum. Let cool.

1-2 cups chopped pecans

1 cup full fat buttermilk

2 tsp good vanilla.

*Mix sugar and oil well. Mix in one egg at a time, add prunes and vanilla. Add in buttermilk.

*In a different bowl mix flour, spice, soda, nuts.

*Stir dry ingredients in wet ingredients.

*Do not use a mixer.

*Pour into a greased tube pan.

*Bake in a tube pan at 325°F for 60 minutes.

Recipe continues on next page >>>>>

Make and cover cooled cake with caramel icing. Recipe follows.

2 cups white sugar divided

1/2 cup for browning + 2 Tbs water.

1 stick cold butter

1/2 tsp salt

1 Tbs flour

1 Tbs white corn syrup

1 small can evaporated milk (5oz) or cream.

*Spray a medium size deep heavy skillet, put in 1/2 cup sugar and water. Then mix ingredients except butter in a bowl and warm in the microwave.

*Let sugar and water brown on medium heat. When golden dark brown add cold butter. When melted add milk mixer. Let come to a rolling boil for 2 minutes (soft boil stage 236). Remove from heat and beat until thick and ready to spread. Spread over cooled cake.

Best severed next day.

Prune Cake Remix

1 box Duncan Hines spice cake mix.

1 cup chopped prunes and 1/2 cup water.

1 box vanilla instant pudding

1/4 cup dark brown sugar

1/4 cup white Lilly flour

1 tsp baking powder

1 tsp allspice

1 tsp cinnamon

1/4 tsp clove

1/2 tsp ginger

1 cup cooking oil

4 eggs

1 Tbs vanilla extract.

*Set oven on 350°F

*Prepare at least 10 cup size bundt or tube pan with spray oil, dust with flour, then spray oil again.

*Microwave the prunes and water for 3 minutes. Let cool then mash to Paste. In a large heavy-duty mixer add oil, eggs, vanilla and mashed prunes. In another large bowl mix dry ingredients then add the dry ingredients to the wet ingredients in the mixer. Mix for 2 minutes. Pour into the prepared baking pan.

*Bake until brown and the top is firmly set for about 50 minutes. I use a cake tester.

Use a container of vanilla store-bought frosting. Beat in one cup of powdered sugar. Spread on completely cooled cake. Stream store bought caramel sauce on top of the cake.

157

Mama's Carrot cake

*Preheat the oven to 350°F

*Prepare 2 deep 9 in. cake pans, 9x13 pan or a tube / Bundt pan with oil and flour. I spray the pans with Baker's Joy. A Tube cake pan does not have ridges.

2 cups self-rising flour+1/4 tsp salt

3 cups grated carrots

1 cup chopped pecans

1 Tbs cinnamon, 1/2 tsp nutmeg, allspice, ginger and nutmeg. 1/4 tsp clove.

2 cups sugar

4 eggs beaten

1 1/2 oil (I use canola)

1 8 oz crushed pineapple drained

1 Tbs vanilla

*Mix dry ingredients together in a large bowl.

*Mix sugar, pineapple, oil, eggs and vanilla. Stir into dry ingredients.

Icing

1/2 block Cream cheese

1 stick Butter

1/4 tsp Salt

1 tsp Vanilla

1 tsp Lemon and orange or lime zest

Or 1/4 tsp Pure lemon extract.

4 cups powdered sugar

*Beat with a mixer until light and fluffy. Spread on completely cooled cake. Best when served the next day. It needs to set for some hours for the best flavor.

Easy Carrot Cake

1 box spice cake mix

1/4 cup flour

1/4 cup dark brown sugar

1 box villa instant pudding

2 cups grated carrots

1 cup chopped pecans

1 tsp baking powder

1 tsp cinnamon

1/2 tsp nutmeg, allspice, ginger and

1/4 tsp clove. Or 1 Tbs pumpkin pie spice. (Dry ingredients)

1 cup cooking oil

4 beaten eggs

1 8 oz crushed pineapple drained

*Mix in a bowl by hand the dry ingredients.

*Mix the wet ingredients in a bowl then hand mix them into the dry.

*Bake in prepared pan.

Frosting

1 can cream cheese frosting.

1 cup powdered sugar

1 tsp vanilla extract

1/2 tsp lemon extract

Spread over the cakes or top and middle layer of completely cooled cake. Let set for 8 hours or overnight for best flavor.

Easy cheesecake

*Heat oven to 325F Put 1 Cup water in oven

Crust

1/2 box butter cake mix -

1/4 cup butter melted.

1 egg

1/4 tsp nutmeg

1/4 cup crushed pecans

Filling

(3) 8 oz packs Philadelphia cream

Cheese room temp.

1/2 Cup sour cream room temp.

(1) 14 can condensed milk.

3 large eggs room temp.

2 Tbs dry cake mix.

1/2 tsp salt

1 Tbs good quality Vanilla extract

1/2 tsp Lemon extract

2 Tbs lemon juice

1 Tbs lemon zest

Strawberry Sauce

Frozen strawberries, strawberry glaze and two Tbs dry strawberry jello. Mix in 1/4 cup boiling water stir well and add to glacé. Mix in frozen strawberries. Add extra sugar if desired

Cool whip and mint leaves

Directions
*Mix crust and press into spring form pan. Bake 6 minutes

Fillings
*Mix cheese, sour cream, milk about 3 minutes.

*Mix in dry cake mix and salt.

*Add one egg at the time. Beat until yolk disappears.

*Add lemon juice and vanilla.

*Pour into crust.

*Bake 1 hour. Turn the oven off and let it sit in the oven 1 hour.

*Remove from the oven and let cool completely.

*Chill in the refrigerator 4 hours or overnight. Make cheesecake at least 1 day before needed.

Old Fashion Fresh Apple Cake

*Pre-heat oven to 325F

*Prepare a large 12 cup tube pan with oil and flour. I use baker's joy.

1 1/2 cup canola oil

1 cups brown sugar

1 white sugar

4 extra large eggs

1/4 cup dark rum or 1/2 Cup

orange juice.

1 Tbs good quality vanilla

1 tsp ground cinnamon

2 tsp ground allspice

1/8 tsp ground cloves

1/4 tsp ground ginger

3 cups White Lilly self-rising flour

1/2 tsp baking soda

3 cups finely chopped firm

Apples like Granny Smith. **Do not peel.**

2 Tbs lemon juice mix in apples

1 cup chopped pecans

1 cup coconut

*Stir oil, sugar, eggs and vanilla in a bowl mix well with a whisk

*In stand mixer, put flour, spice, coconut, pecans and apples mixed with lemon juice. Stir all dry ingredients t together with flour. Mix in wet ingredients into dry ingredients until blended well. Batter will be

thick.

Pour into prepared tub pan. Bake 75 minutes until top is golden brown and set. I use a cake tester. Remove from pan after 15 minutes. Continue to cool. Best served the next day.

Easy Old Fashion Hummingbird Cake

*Heat oven to 350F

(Prepare a large tube pan with oil then flour. I use Bakers Joy

Wet Ingredients

Mash 2 cups ripe bananas (approx 3)

(1) 8 oz can crushed pineapple (1cup) **(Do not drain)**

1 cup white sugar

1 cup brown sugar

3 ex-large eggs room temp.

1 1/2 cup canola oil

1 Tbs vanilla

Dry ingredients

3 cups White Lilly self-rising flour

1/2 tsp baking soda

2 cups chopped pecans divided

(1/2 cup for top)

1 tsp ground cinnamon

2 tsp ground Allspice

1/4 tsp ground cloves

Directions

*Stir wet ingredients together in a large mixing bowl. Blend well with a whisk.

*Stir together in a stand mixer the dry ingredients. Mix wet ingredients into dry mixture blending well. Pour into prepared tube pan. Bake

about one hour until top golden brown and set. I used a cake tester. You may use (2) 9 in layer cake pans. Bake until the top rises up and is set. About 50 minutes.

Remove from oven and let cool 15 minutes. Remove from pan and cool completely.

Prepare Cream Cheese Frosting

(1/2) 8 oz cream cheese pack.

(1/2) stick butter room temperature

4 cups powdered sugar.

1/4 tsp salt

1 tsp vanilla extract

1/2 tsp lemon extract

2 Tbs lemon juice

1 Tbs milk if needed

*Beat with whisk in heavy duty mixer hand mixer five minutes. Should be light and fluffy.

*Cover cake with frosting place pecans on the top. Best served the next day.

Old Fashion Gingerbread Pound Cake

Pre-heat oven to 325F

Prepare a 10-15 cup tube pan with oil then flour. I use Baker's Joy

3 sticks butter, room temp

2 cup dark brown sugar

1 cup white sugar

6 ex-large eggs room temp

1 Tbs good quality Vanilla

1/2 cup Sorghum molasses, (spray measuring cup with oil).

1 cup sour cream, room temp

3 cups White Lilly flour

1 box instant lemon pudding, (I use Kroger brand).

1 tsp baking powder

1/2 tsp salt

1 Tbs ground ginger

2 tsp cinnamon

1/2 tsp ground cloves

1/4 tsp nutmeg

1/4tsp ground allspice

*Cream butter and sugar 5 minutes in heavy mixer. Add vanilla and eggs one at a time. Mix well.

*Mix all dry ingredients together in a mixing bowl stir well. Add sour cream and molasses in a bowl blend well.

*Mix flour mixture alternating with the sour cream mixture beginning and ending with flour mixture until completely blended well.

*Pour into prepared tube pan. Place in oven on a cookie sheet. Bake until top is brown and set about 1 hour to hour and 15 minutes. I use a cake tester that comes out clean.

*Let cake cool for 10 minutes then remove from the tube pan. Let cool completely. Prepare lemon glacé

Lemon Glacé

*Mix 2 cups powdered sugar, 1 Tbs soft butter, 3 Tbs lemon juice and 1 tsp lemon zest, pinch salt. More lemon juice if needed to spread glacé over cake. Let glacé dry. Best served next day.

Mama's Famous Potato Yeast Rolls

The soft light cinnamon pecan yeast rolls mama brought home from work were so good that they would make your bottom lip kiss your top lip. Mama was learning to make these delicious delicate yeast rolls at her new job.

Mama's sisters learned to make yeast rolls working on the place for white families as their maids and cooks. They loved their families that they worked for, and the families loved my aunties. They became experts in making these fragrant soft yeast rolls as they served them to their families several times a week. Mama did not work outside her home while raising her children. She had not mastered the art of making yeast rolls. Even though, she was an excellent cook.

After our youngest sister Kathy was old enough to go to school. Mama got a job working in the kitchen as the pastry cook at the local school cafeteria. The previous pastry cook was charged with teaching her to make all kind of delicious breads. They made everything from scratch in those days. She could make biscuits and cornbread, but she never learned to make these light fluffy yeast breads. After the first week at work Mama tried to make a batch of cinnamon yeast rolls at home. They came out heavy, stiff and not very good. But she did not let that stop her. She went back to work and practiced even harder. Eventually she learned to master these light delicate yeast breads.

One Saturday. I went to a yard sale. I found a large square red and white metal canister that had recipes printed all over it, perfect to store my White Lilly flour. When mama came to my home, she saw the canister with recipes on it and noticed that it was for potato yeast

169

rolls. She took some paper and copied the recipe down. She had never heard of a yeast roll recipe with potatoes in it. I never paid any attention to the recipes on the can. Mama noticed everything and was always ready to try it out. She went home and made this potato yeast roll recipe.

Potato Yeast Rolls

2 packages of yeast
2 cups mashed potatoes (about 2 large potatoes)
1 cup potato water
1 cup shortening (I use butter)
1 cup sugar
1 Tbs salt
3 extra-large eggs beaten
8-10 Cups White Lilly bread flour

Instructions:
*Bloom the yeast in 1/2 cup warm water 110 degrees add 1 tsp sugar and 1 tsp flour. Let sit until it rises up, about 5 minutes. You will be able to smell the yeast aroma.
*Peel and boil the potatoes, when soft drain reserving two cups potato water, mash and let cool.
*Mix warm mashed potatoes, potato water, shortening, sugar, yeast mixture and salt together. They should be warm. But not hot.
*Add the beaten eggs. Mix in 2 cups flour, then mix well. Mix in one cup at a time until a soft dough forms. Let the mixer need the bread about 2 minutes until the dough pulls away from the side of the

mixing bowl.

*Place the dough in 2 large oiled mixing bowls cover loosely with plastic wrap and place in the refrigerator overnight. Next day let rise in a warm place until double in size or mama would say "double in bulk". Then mash the dough down and let it rise again.

*When double in bulk, pour the dough out of the bowl on to a floured surface, mash the dough down and cover the top with flour then roll out with a rolling pins out one inch thick, cut the rolls into shape with a round biscuit cutter or a drinking glass and place the rolls on a large baking sheet pan. Let rise again. Bake them in a 450-degree oven until rich golden brown.

At her job, mama was taught to always used Fleischmann brand yeast, it has a better yeast flavor and White Lilly brand unbleached flour, it is a lighter southern wheat flour that makes the bread lighter. She also used Cisco brand butter flavored shortening because it made the texture of the rolls better than butter. She used a Kitchen Aide heavy duty mixer. Kitchen Aide mixers mix better and do not wear out.

I have found that you can also use a large heavy duty food processor using the bread blade. I use Cuisinart 14 cup capacity.

After her visit with me, she went home and made a batch of potato yeast rolls, they came out perfectly light, moist, fragrant and sweet. She had learned her job well. She taught me how to make them, my sisters Brenda and Debra also learn to make them. I hope that we have someone in the next generation that will be willing to learn to make them.

Mama became famous for her potato yeast rolls. She made them for every holiday and special occasion. She had to make at least two batches for her children because everyone always wanted to take some home. From time to time she made batches and sold them to her family members, neighbors, church members and friends that put in orders for them. She would serve them at her Sunday dinners after church. She took them to family dinners, reunions, parties, weddings, funeral repasses and Church suppers.

When mama was 91, during the Christmas holiday she wanted to make some of her famous potato yeast rolls again, however she was not able to cook anymore so she taught her nurse aide to make them for her. She sat in the wheelchair while the nurse followed her directions. They were real treats. She also taught her nurse aides to bake carrot cake, and Million-dollar pound cake. Mama passed away the next March 2017. Her nurses will never forget all that she taught them. Her children won't forget it either.

Moral of the story. If first you don't succeed, don't give up. Try try again until you get it. And when you learn to make something teach someone else to make it. Nothing beats a failure but a try.

CONCLUSION

I hope that you enjoyed this book, it's stories, it's poems and recipes. It was written for entertainment, fellowship and to share family history. Try the recipes they have been updated to make them easier to make. Look for additional books about the grandchildren, great grandchildren and other generations to come.

Personal Reflections

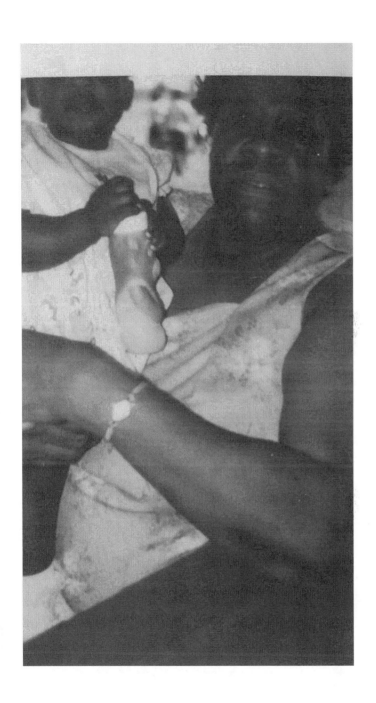

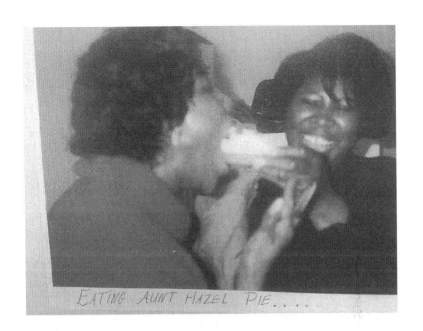

EATING AUNT HAZEL PIE....

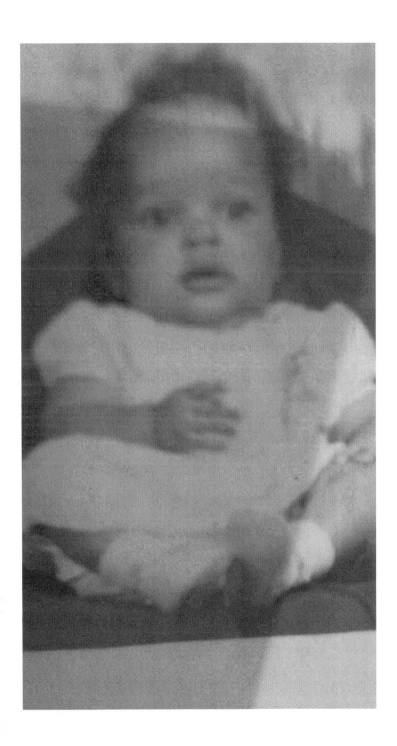

Thank you for purchasing and reading my book!

I hope you enjoyed the stories, words of wisdom, recipes and rich family history. I would be humbled if you were to leave me a **REVIEW ON AMAZON!** Simply scan the **QR Code** below to be taken to my book's Amazon.com page.

Thank you again for the support!

Ann Buchanan

Made in the USA
Columbia, SC
04 April 2024

34001974R00129